HARVARD SEMITIC SERIES

VOLUME III

HARVARD SEMITIC SERIES

VOLUME III

CAMBRIDGE, U.S.A.
HARVARD UNIVERSITY
1912

SUMERIAN TABLETS

IN THE

HARVARD SEMITIC MUSEUM

PART I

CHIEFLY FROM THE REIGNS OF LUGALANDA AND URUKAGINA

OF LAGASH

COPIED

WITH INTRODUCTION AND INDEX OF NAMES OF PERSONS

BY

MARY INDA HUSSEY, Ph. D.

CAMBRIDGE, U.S.A.

HARVARD UNIVERSITY

1912

LEIPZIG, J. C. HINRICHS'sche BUCHHANDLUNG

PRINTED IN GERMANY

EDITORIAL NOTE.

THE Harvard Semitic Series will consist of occasional volumes in the field of Semitic exploration, philology, literature, history, and religion.

Volumes I and II, which are now in preparation, will give the results of the explorations carried on at Samaria in the years 1908—1910.

The present volume by Dr. Hussey comprises those cuneiform tablets belonging to the Harvard Semitic Museum which come from the reigns of the Sumerian rulers Lugalanda and Urukagina. While Sumerian is not a Semitic tongue, its relations to Babylonian and Assyrian are so intimate that the inclusion of a Sumerian volume in a Semitic series will be considered as a matter of course by workers in this field. The tablets here published were acquired by the Museum in the years 1903 and 1904, from two New York dealers.

The cost of the publication of this volume has been met by the generosity of the Hon. Jacob H. Schiff, founder and patron of the Semitic Museum.

The SUMERIAN TABLETS may be ordered from the *Harvard Publication Agent*, Cambridge, Mass., or from the *J. C. Hinrichs'sche Buchhandlung*, Leipzig, Germany. The price is $ 5.00 or 20 Marks, postage prepaid.

CONTENTS.

		Page
Editorial Note	. . . .	V
Contents	. . . .	VII
Abbreviations	. . . .	VIII
Introduction	. . . .	1—11
Register of Tablets	. . . .	12—13
Index of Names of Persons	. . . .	14—36
Texts	. . . . Plates	1—75
Photographic Reproductions	. . . . Plates	76—81

ABBREVIATIONS.

Br. . . . Brünnow, R. E., A Classified List, etc. Leyden, 1889.

DP. . . . La Fuye, Allotte de, Documents Présargoniques, Fasc. I. Part 1, Paris, 1908, Part 2, Paris, 1909.

Nik. Doc. Nikolski, M. V., Documents of Agronomic Reports, etc., St. Petersburg, 1908 (in Russian).

REC. . . Thureau-Dangin, Fr., Recherches sur l'Origine de l'Écriture Cunéiforme, Paris, 1898, Supplément, 1899.

RTC. . . Thureau-Dangin, Fr., Recueil de Tablettes Chaldéennes, Paris, 1903.

TSA. . . Genouillac, H. de, Tablettes Sumériennes Archaïques, etc., Paris, 1909.

INTRODUCTION.

The tablets published in this volume are for the most part accounts of the palace and temple expenses for various months from the fifth year of Lugalanda to the seventh year of Urukagina.[1] The provenance of most of them is assured by the mention of Lagash in the date formula, or, where this is lacking, by their similarity to tablets known to have come from that place.

Of No. 1 probably only about one half of the obverse has been preserved, and the reverse is entirely broken away except the remains of the column lines discernible at the bottom. A line is drawn across the upper margin, thus separating the obverse from the reverse. This tablet contains a list of proper names, and is to be classed palaeographically with Nos. 9—15 of the first series of Thureau-Dangin's *Recueil de Tablettes Chaldéennes*. He has pointed out in his introduction that the frequent use in those tablets of the name of the god of *Šuruppak* as an element in proper names is an indication that they may have come from *Šuruppak*. For the same reason this tablet may also be supposed to have come from that place.

Nos. 2—4 are general statements of monthly expenses.

No. 41 is a list of offerings to the gods.

Nos. 42—52 are of heterogeneous character and have therefore been placed together.

The rest of the tablets belong to groups, or series, designated by the Sumerian scribes as follows:

še-ba lú-šuku(-ku) ba: Nos. 3—13.
dub igi-dub: No. 14.
še-ba igi-nu-dŭ šag-dub-ḫal: Nos. 15—16.
še-ba igi-nu-dŭ il šag-dub-ḫal: Nos. 17—18.
še-ba e-kid-a: No. 19.
še-ba gim-tur ᵈBa-ú: No. 20—23.
še-ba gim-tur il igi-nu-dŭ šag-dub-ḫal: No. 24.
še-ba lú-tur-tur-la-ne: Nos. 25—27.
zid šu-ḫa ú-rum ᵈBa-ú: No. 28.
še-ba šu-ḫa ab-ba: No. 29.
še-nig áš-nig sá-dú(g) itu-da: Nos. 30—36.
še kú-a gud udu: No. 37.
gan šuku ki-a: Nos. 38, 40.
gan ú-rum ᵈBa-ú: No. 39.

---

[1] Publications of other tablets from this period are as follows:
Recueil de Tablettes Chaldéennes, by Fr. THUREAU-DANGIN, 1903.
Documents Présargoniques, by ALLOTTE DE LA FUŸE, Fasc. I, Part 1, 1908, Part 2, 1909.
Tablettes Sumériennes Archaïques, by H. DE GENOUILLAC, 1909.
Documents of Agronomic Reports of the Oldest Epoch of Chaldea from the Collection of N. P. Likhachev, by M. V. NIKOLSKI, 1908 (in Russian).
Oldest Bulls and Seals of Shirpurla, by N. P. LIKHACHEV in "Memoirs of the Classical Division of the Imperial Archaeological Society". Tome IV, 1907 (in Russian).
The Amherst Tablets, by T. G. PINCHES, Part I, 1908.

Copies of the tablets correspond in size to the originals. Shading indicates some defacement of the tablet, either by an injury received while the clay was still soft or by a break that has occurred afterwards. An attempt has been made faithfully to reproduce the original text, but I am aware that, in cases in which the scribes allowed themselves considerable latitude in the number of minute parallel wedges in a given sign, I have not at all times reproduced the exact number. In no case, however, have I exceeded the limits of variation which the scribes allowed themselves, and rarely will the deviation from the original exceed one wedge: e. g. in the signs *lu* and *la* the number of perpendicular wedges on the tablet varies from three to seven or eight, while in the signs *da* and *šu* there are occasionally as many as nine horizontal wedges.

Characters.

The number of signs which occur here for the first time is not large.[1] ⽕ (1 Ob. I¹), ◁▷ (1 Ob. III¹), ⽕ (42 Ob. I¹), are unknown to me. ⽕ (45 Ob. I²) occurs in Nik. Doc. 241 Ob. I¹. The first of these new signs (1 Ob. I¹) suggests Br. 949. Only a part of the third sign (42 Ob. I¹) is to be seen in the photographic reproduction (Plate 77), because the tablet crumbled somewhat after it was copied but before it was photographed. The form of the following signs is more archaic than any with which I am acquainted:

⽕ (1 Ob. IV²) may be an older form of REC. 8, or it might be *šes-mu*.

⽕ (1 Ob. VII¹) is a heightened form of *nam*. For the usual form see 1 Ob. VI².

⽕ (1 Ob. VI³) is similar to REC. 24.

⽕ (1 Ob. V²) may be compared with REC. 45 or REC. 464[2], but identification with either would be precarious.

⽕ (1 Ob. III³, VI⁵, VII²) = REC. 114.

⽕ (1 Ob. I⁴) = REC. 210.

⽕ (1 Ob. VI³) = REC. 341.

⽕ (1 Ob. V⁴), perhaps *dub* + *udu* + *udu*.

Numerical Notation.

Previous investigators have called attention to the fact that, although at this period numerals are usually written in curvilinear characters, they are occasionally written in cuneiform. In other words, numerals are commonly written with the circular end of the stylus, but sometimes with the square or trapezoidal end. They also agree that the numerical value of a character remains the same in whichever way it is written.

The following facts in regard to the use of the curvilinear and the cuneiform notations[3] in these tablets have been noted.

---

[1] The numbering of the columns in this volume follows the order of the text rather than the consecutive order of the columns on the tablet, i. e., the numbering is from left to right on the obverse, from right to left on the reverse until the completion of the detailed portion and the summary, then the sum total which begins at the top of the left hand column of the reverse and continues toward the right, if one column is not sufficient.

[2] See also the last sign of Ob. line 1 in the E. A. HOFFMANN COLLECTION, No. 106, which is regarded by RADAU in his *Early Babylonian History* p. 428 as a variant of REC. 464. The same sign occurs on tablet 6 Obv. 7 of the Dréhem tablets in the Cleveland Public Library, which I expect to publish in the *Journal of the American Oriental Society*, vol. 33.

[3] For discussions of this subject see DE LA FUYE in *Revue d'Assyriologie*, t. 7, pp. 41—47, and in *Journal Asiatique*, Sér. 10, t. 13 (1909), pp. 241—244; DE GENOUILLAC in TSA., pp. LXX—LXXI; NIKOLSKI in Doc., pp. 12, 16, 18; THUREAU-DANGIN in REC. pp. 22, 88—90.

There are a number of tablets[1] in which all the numerals are written in the curvilinear system with the exception of a) The number of the year[2], or

b) The number of the year and the number of the payment of wages or the distribution[3] of grain. These are always written in cuneiform.

Furthermore, the cuneiform is always used in writing the number of qa[4], in giving the age of an animal[5], or in stating that a second[6] or third[7] payment has been made. It is regularly employed in writing the number of asses, sheep, goats, oxen, or *dun* in accounts which give the allotment of food for domestic animals[8].

The use of the double form of notation in the instances mentioned above may perhaps be sufficiently explained by the fact that the differentiation which the two systems afford greatly facilitates the reading. But that differentiation for the sake of greater ease in reading was not the only purpose served by the cuneiform notation is shown by a careful scrutiny of the methods of book-keeping employed. For the sake of clearness we will designate the totals that occur in the detailed portion of the account as detailed totals; the totals which give a classification of the detailed portion upon the basis of sex, wages, adult or minor age, as the summary[9]; and the totals giving the number of persons and quantity of grain as the sum total[10].

The use of the cuneiform system in those monthly accounts[11] in which both forms of notation[12] are employed is as follows:

---

[1] Nos. 5, 6, 7, 17, 19, 20, 25, 27, 28, 29, 37, 38, 39, 40, 43, 44, 46, 47, 48, 49, 50, 51, 52.

[2] It is generally admitted that the horizontal wedge crossed by one or more oblique wedges at the end of the tablet indicates the year of the reign of the patesi or king. See *Journal Asiatique*, Sér. 10, t. 6 (1905), p. 552; *Revue d'Assyriologie*, t. 6, p. 107; Hilprecht Anniversary Volume, p. 122, note 3; Nik. Doc., p. 6; KING, *A History of Sumer and Akkad*, p. 169.

[3] Written *ba-an* and *nig-an* respectively. The suggestion of NIKOLSKI, Doc., p. 12, that they correspond to the months can scarcely be verified in the form in which he makes it.

[4] Nos. 30 Ob. I[9], III[10, 13], IV[7, 8], V[2, 3, 4] | 32 Ob. I[9], Rev. II[3] | 33 Ob. IV[1, 2] | 35 Ob. II[1, 6, 8] [Rev. V[1, 2]] | 36 Ob. II[2, 7, 9] Rev. V[1, 2]. The word qa is never left unexpressed in these documents. DE LA FUYE has demonstrated that the *gur sag-gal* contained 144 qa (see *Revue d'Assyriologie*, t. 7, pp. 36—40, and *Journal Asiatique*, 10ᵉ Sér., t. 13, pp. 238—241). To the examples which he enumerates may be added Nos. 30, 35, and 36 of our texts. For the number of qa written in the curvilinear notation see Nik. Doc. 261, discussed by DE LA FUYE in *Revue d'Assyriologie*, t. 7, p. 39.

[5] As *mu* 2, *mu* 3; see No. 31 Ob. VII[9, 10], Rev. I[3] | 32 Rev. II[4, 5, 8], etc.

[6] As 2 *kam-ma*; see 15 Ob. III[7] | 17 Ob. IV[1, 4, 6], Rev. IV[2, 16] | 18 Ob. III[10] | 20 Ob. VI[1, 16] | 21 Ob. II[5, 9], VI[1], VIII[4] | 22 Ob. II[8, 12], VII[11], IX[4] | 23 Ob. III[12, 15], VI[18], VII[6], IX[12], Rev. I[12], III[10] | 25 Ob. I[4] | 26 Ob. I[4] | 27 Ob. I[4] | 40 Ob. III[18], Rev. III[6].

[7] As 3 *kam-ma*, 22 Ob. VII[15].

[8] See Nos. 30—36.

[9] The column giving the summary begins with *šu-nigin* and follows the detailed portion after an intervening space, if possible.

[10] *gi-an-šu* is hardly to be translated with DE GENOUILLAC (TSA., 11 Rev. VI[1] p. 33, sq.) "En tout, (par) le dieu Šu!". *šu* = *ana* (Br. 7072): *gi* = *napḫaru* (Br. 3220 and MEISSNER *Seltene Assyrische Ideogramme*, 2033): *an* is perhaps to be compared with its use in the following cases; *a-dun-an*, 21 Rev. V[15] | [*dim-g*]*az-an*, 22 Rev. III[6] | *du-a-tar-an*, 26 Rev. I[14] | *lul-an*, 25 Ob. VII[4], 26 Rev. II[3] | *nita-an*, 17 Rev. I[1], 18 Ob. VII[11] | *sal-an*, 17 Rev. I[3], 18 Rev. II[9], 25 Ob. VI[2], 26 Rev. II[5], 27 Rev. II[2], III[2] | *šu-i-an*, 25 Ob. III[16] | *šu-i sal-an*, 25 Rev. I[11], 26 Rev. III[8] | *ú-bil-an*, 22 Rev. II[6], or perhaps even with *kam-ma-an*, 40 Rev. III[6] IV[7], or *ba-an* and *nig-an* preceded by the numerals from one to twelve to indicate the number of the payment. The latter is found at the end of most of the monthly accounts.

[11] Namely, Nos. 8, 9, 10, 11, 12, 13, 15, 16, 18, 21, 22, 23, 24, 26, 30—36.

[12] In the following verifications the correctness of the numbers that have been supplied is assured either by the detailed total or by comparison with a similar account. Arabic numerals have been used for the transliteration of the curvilinear, and Arabic numerals followed by a obelus for the cuneiform.

1) When both forms are employed in the detailed portion, in the summary, and in the sum total, the numbers in the summary and in the sum total are the sums of those numbers written respectively in each form of notation in the detailed portion of the account.

No. 10   Detail   Summary   Sum total

Rev. IV[3] $\left[\frac{2}{4}\dagger\right] =$ Rev. VI[1] 1† at $\left[\frac{2}{4}\right]$ $=$ Rev. VII[1] 1† person
                                     Rev. VII[2] $\frac{2}{4}$† gur

No. 12

Ob. I[10], VI[10] ⎫
Rev. I[3, 7, 9, 11, 13] ⎪
Rev. II[2, 4, 6, 8] $\frac{2}{4}$† $=$ Rev. V[1] 13† at $\frac{2}{4}$ ⎫
Rev. III[5, 9] ⎬   ⎪   Rev. VI[1] 22† persons
Ob. VI[9] $\frac{1}{4}\frac{2}{24} =$ Rev. V[2] 6† at $\frac{1}{4}\frac{2}{24}$ ⎬ $=$ Rev. VI[2] $9\frac{1}{4}$† gur
Ob. V[9, 12] ⎫ ⎪
Ob. VI[1] ⎭ $\frac{1}{4}$†   Rev. V[4] 3† at $\frac{1}{4}$ ⎭

No. 13

Ob. I[9], VI[9] ⎫
Rev. I[[1], 5, 7, 9, 11] ⎪
Rev. II[1, 3, 5, 7] $\frac{2}{4}$† $=$ Rev. V[1] 13† at $\frac{2}{4}$† ⎫
Rev. III[5, 9] ⎬   ⎪   Rev. VI[1] 22† persons
Ob. VI[8] $\frac{1}{4}\frac{2}{24} =$ Rev. V[2] 6† at $\frac{1}{4}\frac{2}{24}$ ⎬ $=$ Rev. VI[2] $9\frac{1}{4}$† gur
Ob. V[7, 10, [13]] $\frac{1}{4}$† $=$ Rev. V[4] 3† at $\frac{1}{4}$ ⎭

No. 23

Rev. VII[10] $\frac{3}{24}$† ⎫
Rev. VIII[8] $\frac{3}{24}$† ⎬ $=$ Rev. IX[9] [2]† at $\frac{3}{24}$ ⎫   Rev. X[1] 4† persons
                      ⎬ $=$
Rev. VIII[9] 2† at $\frac{2}{24}$ $=$ Rev. IX[5] 2† at $\frac{2}{24}$ ⎭   Rev. X[2] $\frac{1}{4}$† $\frac{4}{24}$† gur

No. 26

Ob. I[9] $\frac{2}{4}$†   omitted in Rev. IV[1] ⎫   Rev. V[1] 2† persons
                                  ⎬ $=$
Rev. II[2] $\frac{1}{4}$† $=$ Rev. IV[2] 1† at $\frac{1}{4}$ ⎭   Rev. V[2] $\frac{3}{4}$† gur

2) When the cuneiform is used in the detailed portion and in the summary but not in the sum total, the cuneiform of the summary corresponds to the cuneiform of the detailed portion, and the sum total, which is written in curvilinear, is the sum of those numbers written in curvilinear alone, the cuneiform being entirely omitted, as in Nos. 8 and 16.

No. 8   Detail   Detailed Summary   Detailed Total   Summary   Sum Total

Rev. III[6] $\frac{2}{4}$† $=$ Rev. V[1] 1† at $\frac{2}{4}$ $=$ Rev. VI[1–2] omitted

No. 16

Ob. VII[3] $\frac{4}{24}$† $=$ Ob. VII[12] 1† at $\frac{4}{24}$ $=$ Ob. VII[13] $\frac{4}{24}$† ⎫   Rev. VI[4] 1† at $\frac{1}{4}$ ⎫
Ob. VIII[8] ⎫ ⎪ ⎪
Ob. VIII[9] ⎬ $\frac{4}{24}$† $=$ Rev. III[12] 2† at $\frac{4}{24}$ ⎬ $=$ Rev. IV[1] $\frac{2}{4}$† $\frac{2}{24}$† ⎬   Rev. VI[5] 2† at $\frac{4}{24}$ ⎬ $=$ Rev. VII[1–2] omitted
Rev. I[6] $\frac{1}{4}$† $=$ Rev. III[11] 1† at $\frac{1}{4}$ ⎭   Rev. VI[9] 1† at $\left[\frac{4}{24}\right]$ ⎭

An exception occurs in No. 34 Ob. II[7]—V[15], Rev. V[2], where the quantity of wheat ($a\check{s}$) used in the preparation of certain drinks is the sum of the numbers written in both forms.

	I	$\frac{1}{4}$	$\frac{1}{24}$
Ob. II[7]	9		4
[8]	1†	2†	
III[1]	5†		
[2]		3†	2†
12	5		
13		3	2
IV[13]	2	2	
V[1]		1	4
3	10		
4	1	2	4
6	7	2	
7	1	1	
10		1	
11		1	
12		.	2
	41	18	18	$= 46\frac{1}{4}$ Rev. V[2]

The curvilinear and cuneiform are added together in the detailed total in No. 11 Ob IV[14], but the cuneiform is omitted from the final sum total.

3) Both forms of notation may be used in the detailed portion, in the summary, and in the sum total which gives the number of persons, but the cuneiform may be omitted in the sum total which gives the quantity of grain, in which case the grain total is the sum of the numbers written in curvilinear alone, as is illustrated by the following table.

No. 9	Detail	Detailed total	Summary	Sum total
Rev. IV[1]	$\frac{2}{4}$†		Rev. V[1] 1† at $\frac{2}{4}$ =	Rev. VII[1] 1† person.
				Cuneiform omitted from grain
				total in Rev. VII[2]

No. 15

Ob. VI[16]	$\frac{4}{24}$†			
Ob. VIII[3]	$\frac{4}{24}$†	Ob. VII[6,7]	Rev. V[4] 1† at $\frac{1}{4}$	Rev. VI[11] 4† persons.
Ob. VIII[4]	$\frac{4}{24}$†	= Rev. II[16]	= Rev. V[5] 2† at $\frac{4}{24}$	= Cuneiform omitted from grain
Ob. VIII[13]	$\frac{1}{4}$†	Rev. III[1,6]	Rev. V[9] 1† at $\frac{4}{24}$	total in Rev. VI[12]

No. 18

Ob. VIII[1] $\left[\frac{3}{24}†\right]$ = Ob. VIII[12,13] = Rev. VI[8] 1† at $\frac{3}{24}$ = Rev. VII[1] 1† person.
Cuneiform omitted from grain
total in Rev. VII[2]

In accounts which give the allotment of food for domestic animals[1] there is need of only

---

[1] In this series ($\check{s}e$-nig $a\check{s}$-nig) 30 days are to be reckoned to the month, except in No. 32 Rev. I[10]—III[6], in computing the food for the dun-$gi\check{s}$-gi. Here 32$\frac{1}{2}$ seems to be required, but in Ob. II[3-6] only 30 (!).

one total, namely the grain total. Numbers written in cuneiform may be omitted from this total, as in Nos. 34, 35 and 36.

Verification of barley ($\check{s}e$) used in No. 34.

	I	$\frac{1}{4}$	$\frac{1}{24}$	qa	
Ob. I¹⁰	17	2			
II¹	1	1			
II⁵	5	2	3		
	23	5	3		$= 24 \frac{1}{4} \frac{3}{24}$ grain for asses
Ob. II⁹	5				
II¹⁰	1	2	4		
II¹¹	7	2			
III³	2	2			
III⁴		3	2		
III⁵	2	2			
III⁸	8		3		
III⁹	4		1	3	
III¹⁰	4		1	3	
III¹⁴	2	2			
IV¹		3	2		
IV²	2	2			
IV⁶	1	1			
IV⁷	1	1	5		
IV⁸		1	5		
IV⁹	1	1			
IV¹⁰		2	[3]		
IV¹¹			5		
V⁹		1	1		
	40	25	32	6	$= 47 \frac{2}{4} \frac{3}{24}$ grain for preparation of drinks
Ob. VI⁴	4	2	3		
VI⁷	3	1	3		
VI¹⁰	4		2		
Rev. I⁷	7		1		
I¹⁰	1	1			
I¹⁵	10				
II¹¹	6	1			
III⁷, ⁹, ¹¹, ¹³, ¹⁵ IV³			18		
	35	5	27		$= 37 \frac{1}{4} \frac{3}{24}$ grain for the sheep, etc.

$$109 \frac{1}{4} \frac{3}{24} = \text{Rev. V}^1$$

In making this calculation the cuneiform in Rev. III⁴, i. e. $7 \dagger \frac{2}{4} \dagger \frac{2}{24} \dagger$ gur, has been omitted.

Since Nos. 35 and 36 are entirely similar, the one may be used to supplement the other. Without giving a complete verification, it is to be noted that the following numbers written in cuneiform have been omitted from the total:

No. 35	No. 36
Rev. I[1] .... 6† $\frac{3}{4}$† $\frac{1}{2\frac{1}{4}}$† ...	Rev. I[8]
I[9] .... 10†	I[16]
III[1] .... 8† $\frac{3}{4}$†	III[4]
III[4, 6, 8, 10, 12] $\frac{15}{2\frac{1}{4}}$†	III[7, 9, 11, 13, 15]

4) When both forms are used in the detailed portion, the cuneiform may be omitted from both the summary and the sum total. In this case the totals are the sum of the numbers written in the curvilinear characters in the detailed portion, those written in cuneiform not being counted at all.

Cuneiform omitted in

	Summary	Sum total

No. 14   Detail

Ob. II[3] $\frac{2}{4}$† ⎫ omitted in detailed totals Ob. II[4],
Ob. III[5] 3† at $\frac{1}{4} + \frac{1}{2\frac{1}{4}}$ ⎬ III[6], no sum total being given

No. 21

Rev. VI[4] $\frac{3}{2\frac{1}{4}}$†   = Rev. VII[8] = Rev. VIII[1-2]

No. 24

Rev. II[11] 1† at $\frac{3}{2\frac{1}{4}}$ = Rev. IV[5, 10] = Rev. VI[1-2]
Rev. II[12] 2† at $\frac{2}{2\frac{1}{4}}$

5) Unmistakable signs of erasure show that numbers originally written in cuneiform have been erased and replaced by numbers written in curvilinear.

Erasure of the cuneiform and substitution of the curvilinear are found in No. 11 Ob. I[11], III[10, 11, 13, 14, 16, 17], IV[3, 11, 15], V[2, 3, 5, 6, 8], VI[1, 2, 3, 6, 7], VII[6, 9], Rev. I[2, 6], II[17].

No. 30 Ob. II[3, 6, 7, 8, 9, 13, 14], III[1, 6], IV[6, 8, 9, 11, 12, 13], V[3, 4, 5, 7], VI[1, 2, 8, 9, 10], VII[4, 5, 8, 11], Rev. I[5, 8], II[3, 5, 8, 10, 11], III[3, 6, 7, 11, 12], IV[1, 2].

No. 34 Ob. II[7], III[3, 4, 12, 13], IV[1, 6, 7, 8, 9, 10, 11, 12], V[9], VI[4, 7], Rev. I[10, 13], III[9, 11, 13, 15], IV[3].

For the verification of No. 34 see page 5.

6) In the fourteen pay rolls just considered wages are written in cuneiform 72 times, and in curvilinear 2985 times, i. e., the proportion of the cuneiform to the curvilinear in these tablets is about 1 : 40.[1]

[1] The uses of the cuneiform and curvilinear notations may be tabulated thus:

	Detailed Portion	Detailed Total	Summary	Sum Total
1	cuneiform and curvilinear differentiated	cuneiform and curvilinear differentiated	cuneiform and curvilinear differentiated	cuneiform and curvilinear differentiated
2	"	"	"	cuneiform omitted (note exception)
3	"	"	"	cuneiform and curvilinear differentiated in the sum total of persons, but omitted from the grain total
4	"	cuneiform may be omitted	cuneiform omitted	cuneiform omitted

These facts may be briefly summarised as follows. In accounts in which both notations are used in the detailed portion, the cuneiform could either be noted separately or entirely omitted from the detailed total, from the summary, or from the sum total, or any combination of omission and retention of the cuneiform seems to have been allowable. Its use was restricted, and it was therefore reserved for exceptional cases. In monthly accounts of expense the totals may be expected to represent the amount of disbursement, and amounts that are either not included in the total, or, if included, differentiated from the main total, may very well represent the amounts which for one reason or another were not paid out[1].

The suggestion that wages which were due but unpaid were written in cuneiform and that wages actually paid were written in curvilinear characters may receive some further support from the following consideration. In the tablets published in this volume it is stated some thirty times (see p. 3) that a payment is made twice, and once a payment is made three times. If some monthly accounts show by the writing of the wage in cuneiform that persons have not been paid at all, and others show that the same persons have been paid twice, is it not possible that the latter is a payment of arrears? At present it is impossible to give adequate proof that this is the case. For this it would be necessary to have accounts for consecutive months of successive years. The following table illustrates what is actually found. In Nos. 1 and 3 the double payment precedes the wages written in cuneiform, and in No. 2 the double payment follows the cuneiform, but is separated from it by so long an interval that no necessary connection between the two can be established until the publication of other accounts fills in these intervals.

		Cuneiform	2 Kam-ma
1)	*Mu-ni, sag-engar*	U. 5, 7 *ba-an* (Nik. 20 Ob. V [10])	U. 4, 10 *ba-an* (DP. 117 Ob. V [11])
2)	*É-ta-ĕ, gab-ra-maš*	[U.] 1, 6 *ba-an* (No. 16 Rev. I [6])	U. 3, 10 *ba-an* (No. 17 Rev. IV [2])
		U. 5, 3 *ba-an* (DP. 114 Col. 12 [14—15])	U. 4, 4 *ba-an* (TSA. 14 Rev. IV [4])
			U. 4, 7 *ba-an* (TSA. 15 Rev. IV [5])
3)	*Lugal-ur-mu, gab-rim*	U. 5, 3 *ba-an* (DP. 114 Col. 14 [1])	U. 3, 10 *ba-an* (No. 17 Rev. IV [16])

Clerical Errors.

The accurate and analytic method with which accounts were kept is astonishing. Nevertheless, errors do occur occasionally and may be listed as follows:

1) *nu-nu-[d]ŭ* for *igi-nu-dŭ*, 17 Ob. II [13].
2) *É-ta-dù-ta* for *É-ta-ĕ*, 17 Rev. IV [1].

---

[1] It would be futile to enter into a discussion of the possible causes of lack of payment, for they were probably manifold. The death of a number of persons with whose names we have grown familiar (such as *Lugal-da-nu-me-a, Lugal-dingir-mu, A-bad-mu, Lugal-nanga-ra-ná, E-nam, Ud-ni-kuš,* etc.) is recorded in DP. 138, Nik. Doc. 7, and 14. But cases in which wages of the same person are written in cuneiform in one year and at a later period in curvilinear show that lack of payment must sometimes be attributed to other causes than death, e. g.,

	Wages in Curvilinear	Wages in Cuneiform
Básar	No. 22 Rev. IV [14] = U. 5	TSA. 11 Rev. II [13] = U. 3
	No. 23 Rev. VII [4] = U. 6	
♀ *Baŭzimu,*	No. 22 Rev. V [2] = U. 5	TSA. 11 Rev. II [19] = U. 3
	No. 23 Rev. VII [11] = U. 6	
♀ *Damamu,*	TSA. 12 Rev. IV [16] = U. 5	TSA. 11 Rev. II [17] = U. 3
Étae,	No. 17 Rev. III [20], IV [1] = U. 3	No. 15 Ob. VIII [13] = U pat.
(*gabramaš*)		
♀ *Ezinuamamu,*	No. 22 Rev. IV [18] = U. 5	TSA. 11 Rev. III [8] = U 3

[2] Payments are frequently made in advance in the Orient today.

3) *A-na* for *Za-na*, 21 Ob. V[11].

4) *ᵈMu-mu*[1] for *ᵈŠeš-mu*, 37 Rev. I[2].

5) *Nin-da-nu-me-me* for *Nin-da-nu-me-a*, 22 Ob. IX[6].

6) In No. 11 the detailed total in Ob. VI[15], viz., $2\frac{1}{4}\frac{2}{24}$, is a mistake for $2\frac{2}{4}$. In line 14 both numerals are partly broken away, i. e. the number of men and their rate of wage, [ ] $\frac{2}{24}$. The latter is determined by consulting the summary (Rev. V), which calls for men at three different rates of wage, namely $\frac{2}{4}$, $\frac{1}{4}\frac{2}{24}$, and $\frac{1}{4}$. The rate of wage in line 14 must be therefore $\frac{1}{4}\frac{2}{24}$. The number of men enumerated in the summary who receive this wage is seven. Ob. V[6] mentions one man at this wage, therefore the numeral in line 14 must have been six, since this rate is given in no other line on the tablet.

$$\text{line 13)} \quad 1 \times \frac{2}{4} \qquad = \frac{2}{4}$$
$$\text{line 14)} \quad 6 \times \left[\frac{1}{4}\right] + \frac{2}{24} = \frac{6}{4}\frac{12}{24}$$
$$\overline{\qquad\qquad\qquad \frac{8}{4}\frac{12}{24} = 2\frac{2}{4}}$$

The sum total of $117\frac{2}{24}$ is obtained by adding together the various detailed totals, if this correction is made.

7) In No. 12 Ob. V[2] the scribe has written 2 *gur* instead of 1, i. e., the barley for 4 men at $\frac{1}{4}$ *gur*. This is simply an error in writing down the detailed total, since a verification of the whole account shows the summary and the sum total to be correct.

8) In No. 19 two scribal errors occur: a) in Ob. II[3] where instead of $3\frac{2}{4}$ *gur* there should be only 3 *gur*[2], and b) in Ob. V[2] there should be $1\frac{4}{24}$ instead[3] of $1\frac{2}{24}$. A verification of the summary and sum total[4] show that these are scribal errors and not errors of calculation.

9) In No. 21 the detailed total in Ob. VI[6—10] enumerates 1 *ša(g)-du(g)-nita* and 2 *ša(g)-du(g)-sal*, whereas in the portion of which this is the detailed total (Ob. V[5]—VI[4]) no *dumu nita* is mentioned. A comparison of Ob. V[5]—VI[4] with DP. 112 Ob. IV[18]—V[16] shows the error

---

[1] See No. 37 Ob. II[8], III[6], IV[3], V[9], Rev II[4].

[2] $8 \times \left(\frac{1}{4} + \frac{2}{24}\right) = \frac{8}{4} + \frac{16}{24}$
$1 \times \left(\frac{1}{4} + \frac{2}{24}\right) = \frac{1}{4} + \frac{2}{24}$
$\overline{\qquad\qquad \frac{9}{4} + \frac{18}{24} = 3}$

[3] $2 \times \left(\frac{1}{4} + \frac{2}{24}\right) = \frac{2}{4} + \frac{4}{24}$
$2 \times \frac{1}{4} \qquad\quad = \frac{2}{4}$
$\overline{\qquad\qquad\qquad 1\frac{4}{24}}$

[4] Verification of Summary of No. 19

Men					Women		
$\frac{2}{4}$	$\frac{1}{4}\frac{2}{24}$	$\frac{1}{4}$	$\frac{4}{24}$	$\frac{4}{24}$	$\frac{3}{24}$	$\frac{2}{24}$
1 1 . Ob. III[2]	10 . . Ob. I[1]	2 . . Ob I[2]	1 . . Ob. IV[3]	1 . . Ob.IV[5]	1 . Ob. IV[1]	1 . Ob. IV[6]
1 2 . . . . . [5]	1 1 . . . . [6]	2 . . . . . [3]	1 . . . . V[3]	1 . . . . V[7]	1 . . Rev. I[5]	
1 1 . . . . [7]	8 . . . . II[1]	2 . . . . . [7]	1 . . Rev. I[7]			
1 . . . .IV[9]	1 . . . . . [2]	1 . . . . II[5]				
	5 . . . . . [4]	1 . . . . II[8]				
	6 . . . [7]	1 . . . III[3]				
	1 . . . . . [9]	2 . . . . V[1]				
	2 . . . IV[12]					
35	44	11	3	2	2	1

2

to be in No. 21 Ob. V^{19}, where *dumu-sal* has been written instead of *dumu-nita*. To obtain[1] a sum total of 33 *ša(g)-du(g)-nita* (Rev. VII^5) line 19 must be counted in accordance with the above correction.

10) In No. 22 there seem to be three mistakes: a) in Ob. VI^{13} $\frac{3}{24}$ is an error for $\frac{4}{24}$ if the detailed total in VI^{18} is correct; b) Ob. VI^{16} calls for *dumu-sal* in the detailed total of VI^{19} instead of *dumu-nita*; c) in Rev. I^{11} we should expect 7 *ša(g)-du(g)-sal* instead of 4 (cf. Ob. VIII$^{10, 13}$, IX^{15}, Rev. I$^{2, 5}$). However, 6 seems to have been the number actually employed in the calculation of the detailed total in Rev. I^{12} (!).

11) In the summary of No. 24 Rev. IV^2 the scribe wrote 81 instead of 93 men at $\frac{1}{4}$ *gur*. That this is merely a scribal error and not one of calculation is shown by counting the number of men who received $\frac{1}{4}$ *gur*[2], and by the fact that 93 must have been the number actually employed in making up the sum total of persons and of barley in Rev. VI$^{1-2}$.

(Note 4, p. 9 continued.)

Verification of Sum Total.

Detailed Totals

	I	$\frac{1}{4}$	$\frac{1}{24}$
Ob. I^4	4	1	2
I^8	4		4
II^3 corrected from $3\frac{2}{4}$	3		
II^6	1	3	4
II^{10}	[2	2]	2
III^4	5	3	
III^6	6		
III^8	[5	2]	
IV^1			3
IV^3			4
IV^5			4
IV^6			2
IV^9		2	
V^2 corrected from $1\frac{2}{24}$	1		4
V^3			4
V^7			4
Rev I^5			3
I^7			4
	31	13	44

= $36\frac{2}{24}$ sum total in Rev. IV^2

[1] On account of the broken state of the text we call attention to the following readings in No. 21:
Rev. VII^9 is to be read (5×10) LAL 3,
Rev. VIII^1 = $(3 \times 60) + (5 \times 10)$ LAL 3,
Rev. VIII^2 = (3×10) LAL $\left(1 + \frac{2}{4} + \frac{1}{24}\right)$.

[2]
12 . . . . . Ob. I^1	5 . . . . II^{17}	4 . . . . III^{18}
15 . . . . ^{4}	2 . . . . III^1	2 . . . . IV^3
12 . . . . ^{6}	3 . . . . ^{3}	1 . . . . ^{4}
12 . . . . ^{9}	1 . . . . ^{4}	1 . . . . ^{5}
5 . . . . ^{13}	3 . . . . ^{5}	2 . . . . ^{11}
3 . . . . II^4	2 . . . . ^{9}	1 . . . . V^8
[2] . . . . ^{11}	1 . . . . ^{11}	1 . . . . ^{10}
1 . . . . ^{14}	[1] . . . . ^{13}	1 . . . . . Rev. 1^{11}

12) In No. 29 Ob. I³ $3\frac{1}{4}$ is written in the detailed total instead of $3\frac{2}{4}$. The sum total of $11\frac{1}{4}$ *gur* in Rev. II² is correct.

13)[1] In No. 34 Rev. I¹⁵ a total of 10 *gur* as the monthly feeding at the rate of $\frac{1}{4} + \frac{4}{24}$ *gur* per ox, requires 24 oxen instead of 26 of l. 12. That 26 is a scribal error for 24 is shown a) by a comparison with No. 35 Rev. I⁶⁻⁹ and No. 36 Rev. I¹³⁻¹⁶, b) by the fact that the sum total (Rev. V¹) requires 24 in line 12.

Inventaire des Tablettes de Tello Tome I (1910) by FR. THUREAU-DANGIN, Tome II, Part I (1910), Part II (1911) by H. DE GENOUILLAC did not come into my hands until after the manuscript of the present volume had gone to the printer (September, 1911).

It is now a great pleasure to acknowledge my obligations to those who have made this publication possible. In the first place to the Baltimore Association for the Promotion of the University Education of Women, whose fellowship I held in the year 1909—1910, and to the Association of Collegiate Alumnae, which granted me the Alice Freeman Palmer Memorial Research Fellowship for the year 1910—1911. During the year 1909—1910 I worked chiefly upon tablets from the Dynasty of Ur, the publication of which I hope may not be long delayed, and during 1910—1911 upon those composing this volume. The latter being older, it seemed proper that they should be published first. To Professor David Gordon Lyon, curator of the Harvard Semitic Museum, I am under no less obligations for allowing me to study and copy the tablets and for many other courtesies.

---

[1] In the detailed total Rev. I⁹ of No. 33 the numeral has been omitted. But since it was not counted in making up the sum total, its omission was probably intentional, in which case it could not be considered an error. (For the omission of numerals written in cuneiform see pp. 5—7.) The errors made in the detailed totals in accounts in which the final totals are correct, or the omission of detailed totals where they might be expected, show that the sum total was not made up from the addition of the detailed totals.

REGISTER OF TABLETS.

Measurements are given in centimeters, length×breadth×thickness, the largest measurements being given. *Ba-an* = payment(?): *gar-an* = distribution(?): *L. pat.* =: *Lugalanda patesi:* *U.* = *Urukagina lugal:* *U. pat.* = *Urukagina patesi.*

TEXT	PLATE	KING	YEAR	MONTH	BA-AN	MUSEUM NO.	SIZE
1	1					3618	9.4×13.5×2.9
2	1	U.	4			3727	5.8× 5.9×2.7
3	2	U.	2	AMAR-A-SI(G)-GA	5 & 12	3570	7.3× 7.1×2.5
4	2	U.	5			3659	6.7× 6.7×2.5
5	3-4	U. pat.	1	EZEN ᵈBA-Ú		3653	11.6×11.7×2.8
6	5-6	U. pat.	1	[EZ]EN-[BU]LUG-KÚ ᵈNINA	2	3568	12 ×12 ×2.6
7	7-8	U.	2	[ ] ᵈNIN-GIR-SU	2	3654	12.7×12.8×3
8	9-10	U.	3	[ ] ᵈNINA	1	3566	12.3×12.7×3
9	11-12	U.	3	SÌG ᵈBA-Ú E-TA-GAR-RA-A	3	3620	12.2×12.2×2.8
10	13-14		3	EZEN ᵈBA-Ú	4	3613	12.3×12.7×3
11	15-16	U.	3	EZEN-BULUG-KÚ ᵈNINA	(10?)	3651	13.5×13.3×3.2
12	17-18	U.	6 (?)		11	3621	11.2×11.3×2.3
13	19-20	U.	6		10	3608	10.7×10.9×2.5
14	21	U.	6			3658	7.7× 7.6×2.5
15	22-23	U. pat.	1	HÁR-RÁ-NE-MÚ-A	5	3719	14 2×14.3×2.8
16	24-25		1		6	3606	12.5×12.6×2.7
17	26-27	U.	3	EZEN ÉŠ-È-LAGAŠᴷᴵ	10	3614	12 6×12.6×2.8
18	28-29	U.	6		12	3619	12 ×12.2×2.5
19	30		4			3722	9.7× 9.7×3.5
20	31-32	U. pat.		SÌG-BA-A	8	3612	12.7×12.9×2.8
21	33-34	U.	2 (?)	EZEN-BULUG-KÚ ᵈNIN-GI[R-SU]	(9?)	3718	15 3×15.2×3.4
22	35-36	U.	5	GÚR-IM-GAB-A	4	3616	13.5×13.4×2.5
23	37-38	U.	6		12	3605	14.2×14.2×3.2
24	39-40	U.	6		11	3615	12.9×12.9×2.6
25	41-42	U.	2	EZEN ᵈBA-Ú		3623	11.5×11.5×2.8
26	43-44	U.	3	UDU-ŠÚ-ŠE-A [ᵈᴵ] NINA TIL-LA-BA	5	3721	11.1×11.1×2.8
27	45-46	U.	3	EZEN ᵈBA-Ú	12	3567	10.7×10.7×2.7
28	47-48	U.	4 (?)			3723	9.1× 9.1×2.6
29	47-48	U.	4		4	3571	6.4× 6.3×2.8
30	49-50	L. pat.	7	ŠE-KIN-KUD-DU	1	3611	13.4×13.4×3.1
31	51-52	U. pat.	1	EZEN-BULUG-KÚ [ ]	9	3652	12.2×12.2×2 5

TEXT	PLATE	KING	YEAR	MONTH	NIG·AN	MUSEUM NO.	SIZE
32	53–54	U.	1	UDU-ŠU-ŠE-A ᵈNIN-GIR-SU	3	3657	10.7×10 7×2.7
33	55–56	U.	4 (?)	EZEN ŠE-KÚ ᵈNINA TIL-LA-BA	2	3622	11.4×11.5×2.7
34	57–58	U.	4	EZEN ᵈNE-(U)GÚN	8	3610	10.6×10.6×2.7
35	59–60	U.	5		5	3656	11.1×11.1×2.6
36	61–62	U.	5		6	3655	10.4×10.5×2.4
37	63–64		4	[ ]-TA-GAR-RA		3720	9.8×10.2×2.5
38	65–66					3609	10.6×10.5×2.8
39	65–66	U.	1			3724	6.9× 6.9×2.4
40	67–68	U.	1			3607	14.8×14.9×3.5
41	69	U.	4			3569	9.4× 9.6×2.7
42	70–71					3617	11 8×11.9×2.8
43	72		3			3730	4.6× 4.6×2.1
44	72		6			3729	5 × 5 ×2
45	72			NIK-KA-ÍD-KA		3573	4.6× 4.6×2.2
46	73	L. pat.	6	ŠE-KIN-KUD-DU		3725	6.2× 6.5×2.5
47	73	U.	7			3731	4.6× 4 6×2.3
48	74		5	EZEA ŠE-KÚ ᵈNINA		3572	4.5× 4.5×2.1
49	74		3	GÀ-ŬR		3732	4.5× 4.5×2
50	74		6	GÀ-UDU-ÚR		3733	4.3× 4.3×2.2
51	75	L. pat	5			3726	6.2× 6.1×2.5
52	75	U.	2			3728	5.7× 5.5×2.3

INDEX OF NAMES OF PERSONS.

It has not been possible to make a detailed study of Sumerian proper names. The index has been prepared for the convenience of those who may use this volume, but it does not purport to indicate the meaning of the names nor to give their correct pronunciation. In general the same system of transcription has been employed as in Thureau-Dangin's *Inscriptions de Sumer et d'Akkad.*

Feminine names are preceded by the sign of Venus. Under all proper names the occupational names are arranged alphabetically and numbered. The word "over" signifies that the person in question is an overseer or foreman; the word "under" means that he is a laborer under the foreman whose name and occupation immediately follow, if they are mentioned on the tablet.

The first numeral in each reference indicates the number of the tablet in this volume, the Roman and superior numerals indicate the column and line respectively. An asterisk before a reference indicates that some part of the line is broken. Names that have been supplied are enclosed in brackets.

Abbreviations: b. = brother; ᵈ = determinative with the name of deity; d. = daughter, dd. = daughters; f. = father; L. = Lugalanda; m. = mother; Ob. = Obverse; prob. = probably; REC. = Thureau-Dangin, *Recherches sur l'origine de l'écriture cunéiforme*; Rev. = Reverse; s. = son, ss. = sons; U. = Urukagina; var. = variant; w. = wife.

A

Á-ág-gà-ni
    il, 15 Ob. IV² | *16 Ob. IV⁴
A-ba-sá
    dup-sar, 6 Ob. V⁵ | 7 Rev. I⁹ | *8 Rev.III⁸ |
    9 Rev. IV³ | 10 Rev. IV⁵ | [11 Rev.
    III⁷] | 12 Rev. III⁹ | 13 Rev. III⁹ | 31 Rev.
    II⁹ | 37 Rev. V⁴ | 38 Ob. IV⁴ | 40
    Rev. V²
A-bád-mu
    sag-engar, 25 Ob. I⁶ | [26 Ob. I⁶] | *27
    Ob. I⁶
A-da-ba
    lul, *15 Rev. II¹¹ | 16 Rev. III⁶
A-da-gal-sá
    qa-šu-dù in service of *Gimtarsirsir,* *25 Ob.
    V⁸ | *26 Ob. V⁵ | *27 Ob. VI¹³
A-dingir-mu
    1) *qa-šu-dù* in service of *Aenramugi,* 25
    Ob. VII¹² | *26 Rev II¹² | [27 Rev. II¹⁴]
    2) *lú-úr,* 40 Ob. VI¹⁶

A + en-ni-ki-ág
    19 Rev. II²
A + en-ra-gin var. (?) *A + en-ra-mu-gi* (q. v.)
    s. (?) of *U.,* *43 Ob. II²
A + en-ra-mu-gi
    s. of *U.,* 25 Rev. II⁵ | *26 Rev. III¹⁴ | [27
    Rev. IV¹¹]
A-gil-sa
    ú-bil, 21 Rev. II⁵
♀ *A-gil-sa*
    in service of *Gimtarsirsir,* 19 Ob. V⁷ |
    25 Ob. VI¹ | *26 Ob VI⁵ | *27 Rev. II¹
A-gir-gal
    in service of *Aenramugi,* *25 Rev. I⁵ |
    26 Rev. III² | *27 Rev. III⁵
A-gub-ná
    1) *sag-dub* of *ki-sìg,* m. of one d., 21 Ob
    I⁷ | 22 Ob. I¹¹
    2) *ki-sìg,* *23 Ob. III¹

A-ḫa-igi
  under *Urmut*, *21 Rev. I⁴

A-ḫum-[ba]
  sag-engar, *27 Ob. V⁹

A-lù-lil-la
  šu-ḫa, *28 Ob. IV⁵

♀ *A-na-ni*
  1) *gim sá-dú(g)*, m. of one d., *22 Ob. VIII⁹
  2) under *Mašdu dupsar*, 20 Ob. VI⁸ | m. of one d., 21 Ob. VIII¹³

Á-ni-kur-ra
  1) title omitted but prob. *sag engar*, *8 Ob. V⁷ | 9 Ob. V¹² | 10 Ob. V¹⁰ | 11 Ob. V⁵ | 39 Ob. II¹ | 49 Ob. II³
  2) *sag-engar*, 5 Ob. II⁵ | 6 Ob. II⁸ | *7 Ob. V² | 12 Ob. V³ | 13 Ob. V²

A-ᵈNina-ki-ág
  [*sag*]-*engar* in service of *Šaḫ-Bau*, *27 Ob. I¹²

A-[sib]-da-ri
  dū-a-tar in service of *Šaḫ-Bau*, *26 Rev. I¹³

♀ *A-ur-mu*
  sal é-gal-la in service of *Gim-Bau*, 25 Ob. III⁶ | *26 Ob. III³ | *27 Ob. III¹¹

Ab-ba
  nim, 15 Rev. II¹ | 16 Rev. II¹³

♀ *Ab-ba-nir-gal*
  ki-gú, 23 Rev. II⁹

Ad-da
  1) 1 Ob. VI⁵
  2) *dìm-gaz*, [20 Rev. I⁹] | *21 Rev. III² | 22 Rev. III⁵ | *23 Rev. V¹⁶

Ad-da-da
  šu-ḫa, *28 Ob I⁵

♀ *Ag-ga-ga*
  1) under *Urmut*, *21 Rev. I⁶
  2) *gim bar-bi-gál* under *Urmut*, *22 Ob. IX¹¹
  3) *sag-dub* of *ki-sìg*, 20 Ob. IV⁴ | 21 Ob. V⁵ | *22 Ob. V⁷

♀ *Al-mu-ni-ka*
  1) *gú-ba*, 22 Ob. IV¹⁹
  2) *ki-sìg*, 23 Ob. V¹⁵

♀ *Ám-ma*
  1) *sag-dub* of *ki-sìg*, 20 Ob. IV⁵ | 21 Ob. V⁷ | 22 Ob. V¹⁸
  2) *ki-sìg*, 23 Ob. II²

♀ *Ama-ᵈAb-sa-é(?)-ta*
  ki-sìg, *23 Ob. VI⁵

♀ *Anna-bár-gi*
  ki-sìg, 23 Ob. VII¹⁷

♀ *Ama-bi-a-gub-ná*
  1) *ki-sìg*, 23 Ob. VI¹⁵ | 23 Ob. VIII¹²
  2) *ki-sìg*, m. of two dd., 23 Ob. V⁴
  3) *sag-dub*, m. of two dd., *22 Ob. III¹⁸
  4) *sag-dub* of *ki-sìg*, m. of one s. and three dd., 20 Ob. I¹⁰ | 21 Ob. III¹⁵

♀ *Ama-da-nu-sá*
  under *Mašdu dupsar*, 20 Ob. VII²

♀ *Ama-en-tud*
  ki-sìg, 23 Ob. IX⁸

♀ *Ama-sal-me-tùg*
  ki-sìg, 23 Ob. IX⁶

♀ *Ama-šág-ga*
  1) *ki-sìg*, 23 Ob. VIII⁶ | m. of one d., *23 Ob. V⁶
  2) *sag-dub* of *ki-sìg*, m. of one d., 20 Ob. I¹³ | 21 Ob. III¹⁸ | *22 Ob. IV²

♀ *Ama-tur*
  gim bar-bi-gal under *Urmut igi-dub*, 22 Ob. IX¹⁶

♀ *Ama-ur-mu*
  sal é-gal-la in service of *Gim-Bau*, 25 Ob. III⁷ | *26 Ob. III⁴ | *27 Ob. III¹²

Amar-ᵈEn-zu
  ad-ge, 40 Ob. V¹⁵

Amar-ezen
  1) 17 Rev. III⁵
  2) *gal-uku*, 9 Ob. I¹¹ | 10 Ob. I⁹
  3) over *giš-túg-pi-kar-rá*, 7 Ob. VII⁷ | *8 Ob. VII⁶ | 9 Ob. VII¹⁶ | 10 Ob. VII¹² | 11 Ob. VII⁷
  4) over *igi-nu-dŭ*, *17 Ob. II¹⁴
  5) over *má-láḫ*, 7 Ob. VII² | [8 Ob. IV¹⁴] | [9 Ob. IV¹⁹] | *10 Ob. IV¹⁶ | 11 Ob. IV⁹
  6) *nagar*, *40 Ob. VI⁵

Amar-ᵈEzinu
  sā, 40 Rev. V⁴ | 45 Ob. I³

Amar-ᵈEzinu-gid-šú
  gala, *18 Rev. II¹⁶ | *24 Ob. V¹⁰

Amar-ḫa-a-ki
  šu-ḫa-a du(g)-ga, *7 Ob. IV⁷ | *8 Ob. VI² | 9 Ob. VI⁹ | 10 Ob. VI⁸ | *11 Ob. VI²

Amar-ki
  1) over *gìn-nita*, 7 Ob. III¹ | 8 Ob. III⁵ | *9 Ob. III⁸ | [10 Ob. III⁶] | 11 Ob. II¹⁵
  2) *šagan-bil*, *33 Rev. IV⁴

Amar-kiš^{ki}
  1) *dup-sar*, *6 Ob. V⁶ | 7 Rev. I¹¹ | 8 Rev.

III¹⁰ | 9 Rev. IV⁵ | *10 Rev. IV⁷ | *11
Rev. III⁹ | 12 Rev. III¹⁰ | 13 Rev. III¹⁰

2) *lù-kas + gar*, 5 Ob. III¹⁰ | 6 Ob. IV⁹ |
7 Rev. IV² | 8 Rev. I³ | 9 Rev. I¹¹ |
*10 Rev. I⁹ | *11 Rev. I⁵ (Title is
omitted but certainly the same man) |
12 Rev. I⁸ | 13 Rev. I⁶ | [20 Rev. I¹⁴] |
*21 Rev. III⁷ | 22 Rev. III¹¹ | 23 Rev.
VI¹ | 24 Rev. I¹⁴ | *25 Rev. I⁷ | *26 Rev.
III⁴ | [27 Rev. III⁷] | *30 Ob. III³ | *31
Ob. III³ | *32 Ob. III⁷ | *33 Ob. III¹¹ |
34 Ob. III⁷ | 35 Ob. III³ | *36 Ob. III⁶ |
40 Ob. VII¹⁸ | 48 Rev. I²

3) *mu*, *5 Ob. V³ | *6 Ob. V¹⁴ | 7 Rev. II⁵ |
[8 Rev. I¹⁶] | 9 Rev. II⁹ | 10 Rev. II¹¹ |
11 Rev. II² | 12 Rev. II⁴ | 13 Rev. II³ |
38 Ob. IV⁹ | 40 Ob. VII⁸

Amar-ᵈTüg-nun
1) over *šu-ḫa*, *28 Rev. I⁵, ⁶
2) over *šu-ḫa ab-ba*, 29 Ob. II⁶

An-a-mu
1) 51 Ob. I³
2) over *nu-sar*, *7 Ob. V¹ | 12 Ob. VI¹² |
*13 Ob. VI¹¹ | 15 Ob. I⁴ | [16 Ob. I⁴] |
17 Ob. I⁶ | 18 Ob. I³ | 19 Ob. I⁵ | 24
Ob. I¹⁰ | 34 Rev. III⁷

An-al-šag var. *An-al-šag-ga* (q. v.)

šu-i, 16 Ob. VII¹ | 17 Ob. VIII¹⁷ | 18 Ob.
VII¹³ | 24 Ob. III¹¹

An-al-šág-ga var. *An-al-šag* (q. v.)
šu-i, 15 Ob. VI¹⁴

♀ *An-da-ti-e*
1) *gim ✕ gug + dìm*, 22 Rev. III¹⁵
2) *ki-sìg*, 23 Ob. I¹⁵

♀ *An-gid-dù*
ki-sìg, 23 Ob. VIII⁸

An-igi-gub
1) *giš-túg-pi-kar-rá* in service of *A + en-
nikiag*, 19 Rev. I⁷
2) *lù-alan*, 17 Rev. I⁷ | 18 Ob. VIII⁴ |
*24 Ob. III¹³

♀ *An-ma-ni-bàr (?)-ba*
ki-sìg in service of *Šaḫ-Bau*, *26 Rev. I¹

An-sib
gab-ra gud-tur-tur, *15 Rev. I¹³ | 16 Rev. II⁹

An-šes-mu
lid-ku, 5 Ob. II¹³ | [6 Ob. III⁴] | *7 Ob.
V¹⁰ | 37 Ob. I⁶, II⁸, III⁶, IV³, [IV¹²],
V⁹, Rev. I²(!), *II⁴ | 38 Ob. II⁸

♀ *Áš-ni-ib*
1) *ki-sìg*, 23 Ob. V¹¹
2) *sag-dub* of *ki-sìg*, 20 Ob. II¹¹ | 21 Ob.
IV⁷ | *22 Ob. IV⁹

♀ *Azag-gi-pad*
w. of *Dudu dupsar*, 40 Rev. II¹⁴

B

♀ *Ba-ba-e*
sag-dub of *ki-sìg*, 20 Ob. III¹⁴

Bá-bá-gà-ni-dug
qa-šu-dù, *15 Ob. V¹⁸ | *16 Ob. VI³ | *17
Ob. VII²

♀ *Ba-ri(g)-gi*
ki-sìg, 21 Ob. VI¹³

♀ *Bá-sar*
gim dun-nig-kù-a, 20 Rev. III¹³ | 21 Rev.
IV¹⁷ | 22 Rev. IV¹⁴ | 23 Rev. VII⁴

♀ (?) *Bá-ša-ma-ma*
over *gim-ḫar*(?), 21 Rev. III¹²

♀ ᵈ *Ba-ù-ama-mu*
1) *gim bar-bi-gál* under *Urmut*, m. of one
s., 22 Ob. IX¹²
2) *ḫar-tud*, 17 Ob. VIII⁷ | 18 Ob. VI¹⁵
3) *il*, 18 Ob. *IV¹, VI¹⁵

4) under *Mašdu dupsar*, m. of one s., *20
Ob. VI¹¹
5) under *Urmut*, m. of one s., *21 Ob.
IX¹³

♀ ᵈ *Ba-ù-babbar-mu*
under *Urmut*, 21 Rev. I⁹

♀ ᵈ *Ba-ù-dim-a-ba-šág*
1) *sag-dub* of *ki-sìg*, m. of one s., 20 Ob.
IV¹¹ | m. of one d., *21 Ob. V¹⁵
2) under *Amar-kiškⁱ*, m. of 1 s., 22 Rev.
II¹² | 23 Rev. V⁹

♀ ᵈ *Ba-ù-dingir-mu*
1) *gim sá-d[úg]*, 22 Ob. VIII¹⁴
2) *šu-i* in service of *Gim-Bau*, 25 Ob. III¹⁵ |
*26 Ob. III¹²
3) under *Mašdu dupsar*, 21 Ob. VIII¹⁸ |
m. of one s., 20 Ob. VI¹⁵

♀ ^d*Ba-ù-ig-gal*
  1) *gim dun-nig-kú-a*, m. of one d., *20 Rev. III¹⁸ | *21 Rev. V⁶
  2) *gim sá-dúg*, 22 Ob. VIII¹⁷ | 23 Rev. III¹¹

[^d*Ba-ú]-lù-[šá(g)]-ga*
  qa-šu-dù, 17 Ob. VII¹

♀ ^d*Ba-ù-lù-šá(g)-ga*
  ḫar-tud, 17 Ob. VIII⁶ | 18 Ob. VI¹⁴

♀ ^d*Ba-ù-lù-ti*
  under *Amar-kiš^{ki} lù-kas + gar*, 20 Rev. I²

♀ ^d*Ba-ù-na-nam*
  ki-sìg, *21 Ob. VII⁹

♀ ^d*Ba-ù-ni-kuš*
  1) *gim ḫubur × gúg + dìm*, 21 Rev. III¹⁹ | 22 Rev. III¹⁴
  2) *ki-sìg*, 23 Ob. I⁶

^d*Ba-ù-ni-su*
  udu-nig-kú-a ba-láḫ-gi-šú, 18 Rev. II¹

♀ ^d*Ba-ù-ur-mu*
  gim dun-nig-kú-a, m. of one d., 21 Rev. V¹¹

♀ ^d*Ba-ù . . . . . -mu*
  ki-sìg in service of *Gimtarsirsir*, 27 Ob. VI⁶

♀ ^d*Ba-ù-zi-mu*
  1) *gim dun-nig-kú-a*, m. of two dd., 21 Rev. V¹ | m. of one s. and one d., *22 Rev. V² | 23 Rev. VII¹¹
  2) *il*, *15 Ob. V⁸ | *16 Ob. V¹⁰

♀ *Babbar-ama-mu*
  ki-sìg, m. of one s. and one d., 21 Ob. VI²²

Babbar-igi-gub var. ^d*Babbar-igi-gub-lugal-an-da* (q. v.)
  1) *dù-a-tar* in service of *Gimtarsirsir*, *26 Ob. V¹⁶ | [27 Rev. I¹¹]
  2) *il*, 18 Ob. IV¹¹

^d*Babbar-igi-gub-lugal-an-da*
  il, 15 Ob. III¹³ | 16 Ob. III¹²

Babbar-lù-mu
  ni-dù, 17 Rev. III¹³

^d*Babbar-lù-šá(g)-ga*
  1) *dun garaš*, i. e., s. of *Girnibaku*, *40 Ob. III¹⁰
  2) *il*, *15 Ob. III¹⁶ | 16 Ob. IV¹ | 17 Ob. V¹²

Babbar-[m]u-kuš
  sag-engar in service of *Gim-Bau*, *27 Ob. I¹¹

Babbar-ni-kuš
  sag-engar in service of *Gim-Bau*, 25 Ob. I⁵ | *26 Ob. I⁵ | *27 Ob. I⁵

♀ *Bár-nam-tar-ra*
  w. of *L.*, 30 Rev. VII⁴ | 46 Rev. II² | 51 Ob. II⁵

♀ *Bár-ud-su(d)-šu*
  1) *gú-ba*, [22 Ob. II¹⁷]
  2) *ḫar-tud*, 18 Ob. VII¹

Bár-zi var. *Bár-zi-ša(g)-gál* (q. v.)
  igi-dub, *7 Rev. IV⁷ | 10 Rev. II³

♀ *Bár-zi*
  over *gim-ḫar*, 21 Rev. III¹⁶

Bár-zi-ša(g)-gál
  1) *igi-dub*, *8 Rev. I⁶ | 9 Rev. II¹ | *11 Rev. I⁶
  2) *lù-kas + gar*, 15 Ob. VIII¹¹ | *16 Rev. I⁴

Bi-su-gà
  lù-sinig, *17 Rev. VI⁶ | 19 Ob. V³

♀ *Bi-su-gà*
  1) *ki-sìg*, 23 Ob. III²
  2) *sag-dub* of *ki-sìg*, 21 Ob. II¹³ | [22 Ob. I¹⁸]
  3) under *Mašdu*, *21 Ob. IX⁶

D

♀ *Da-na*
  sag-dub of *ki-sìg*, 21 Ob. IV¹¹ | m. of one d., 22 Ob. III¹² | 23 Ob. I²

♀ *Dam-a-mu*
  1) *gim dun-nig-kú-a*, 23 Rev. VII¹⁰ | m. of one d., 20 Rev. III¹⁶ | m. of two dd., 21 Rev. IV²¹ | m. of one s. and one d., 22 Rev. IV²⁰
  2) *ki-sìg*, m. of one d., *21 Ob. VI¹⁸ | *22 Ob. VI¹⁵ | 23 Ob. I⁹

Dam-dingir-mu
  1) title omitted but prob. *šub-lugal*, 12 Ob. II⁰ | 14 Rev. I³ | 40 Ob. IV⁴

  2) over *gìn-nita*, 5 Ob. II¹ | *6 Ob. II² | *7 Ob. III⁵ | *8 Ob. III⁷ | 9 Ob. III¹¹ | 10 Ob. III⁹ | 11 Ob. III³ | *38 Ob. I⁸
  3) *šub-lugal*, 13 Ob. III¹

♀ *Dam-ur-mu*
  ki-sìg, 23 Ob. I⁷

♀ *Dìm-^dBa-ù-mu-tud*
  il, *15 Ob. IV⁴ | 16 Ob. IV⁶

♀ *Dìm-^dNina-mu-tud*
  il, *15 Ob. IV⁸ | 16 Ob. IV¹⁰ | 17 Ob. V¹

♀ *Dìm-ᵈNinni-da-gal-sá* var. *ᵈNinni-da-gal-sá*
   (q. v.)
   il, *15 Ob. IV⁵ | *16 Ob. IV⁷ | 18 Ob. IV¹⁴
Dìm-ᵈNinni-ra-gub
   il, *15 Ob. IV¹ | *16 Ob. IV³
♀ *Dìm-ᵈNinni-ra-gub*
   sag-dub of *ki-sìg*, 20 Ob. IV¹⁰
♀ *Dìm-zi(d)-mu*
   il, *15 Ob. V⁹ | *16 Ob. V¹¹ | *17 Ob. VI¹⁰
Du-du
   1) *dup-sar*, 40 Rev. II¹⁵
   2) *sangu*, 30 Ob. VII¹ | 31 Ob. V¹ | 32
      Ob. V¹¹

Dub-dū-da
   *1 Ob. III³
Dub-é-ša(g)-ga
   il, 18 Ob. II⁴
Dub-udu + udu(?)
   *1 Ob. V⁴
Dú(g)-ud-zi
   ad-ge, 40 Ob. V¹⁴
Dun-ᵈEn-lil-li
   lù é-ša(g)-ga, 18 Ob. VI¹⁰
Dun-ša(g)-kuš
   zadim, 18 Rev. I³

E

♀ *É-azag*
   1) *ki-sìg*, 23 Ob. III¹³, ¹⁴
   2) *sag-dub* of *ki-sìg*, 21 Ob. II⁷, ⁸ | 22
      Ob. II¹⁰, ¹¹
♀ *É-bár*
   ki-sìg, 23 Ob. VII¹⁵
♀ *E-da-nam*
   il, *17 Ob. VI¹¹ | 18 Ob. IV¹⁷
♀ *É-dug-li* var. *É-dug-li-su(d)* (q. v.)
   sag-dub of *ki-sìg*, m. of one s., 21 Ob.
      II², ⁴
♀ *É-dug-li-su(d)*
   1) *ki-sìg*, m. of one s., 23 Ob. III⁹, ¹¹
   2) *sag-dub* of *ki-sìg*, m. of one s., 22 Ob.
      II⁵, ⁷
É-dug-nun-sá
   1) *edin*, 38 Ob. III⁹
   2) *sag-engar* in service of *Gim-Bau*, *27
      Ob. I¹⁰
É-dú(g)-si-sá
   over *šu-ḫa-a dug-ga*, 12 Ob. III¹ | 13 Ob. III⁴
É-gil-sa
   ú-bil, [20 Ob. VIII⁴] | 21 Rev. II⁵ | 22 Rev.
      II⁵ | 23 Rev. V³
É-igi-il
   šu-ḫa, *28 Rev. I²
É-ᵈIm-gi(g)ᵏᵘ
   lù-igi + lagab in service of *Gim-Bau*, *25
      Ob. II¹¹ | *26 Ob. II¹⁰ | 27 Ob. III³
É-ki
   sib-anšu, 17 Rev. IV²⁰
É-ki-bi-gí
   šu-ḫa, *28 Rev. I³

♀ *E-ki-bi-gi*
   gim dun-nig-kú-a, m. of two ss., 20 Rev.
      III¹⁴ | m. of two ss. and 1 d., 21 Rev.
      IV¹⁸.
♀ *É-ki-láḫ-mu*
   sag-dub of *ki-sìg*, m. of one s. and two dd.,
      21 Ob. I⁹ | [22 Ob. I¹³] | m. of two ss.,
      23 Ob. II¹⁵
É-me-lám-sud
   šub-lugal, 5 Ob. I⁵ | *6 Ob. I⁶ | 7 Ob. II⁵ |
      *8 Ob. II¹⁴ | *9 Ob. III² | *10 Ob. III¹ |
      11 Ob. II⁷ | *38 Ob. I⁴
É-na-ki
   1 Ob. II²
É-nam
   šub-lugal, *8 Ob. II⁸ | 9 Ob. II⁹ | *10 Ob.
      II⁹ | [11 Ob. II¹]
É-ni-gá-sud
   over *šu-ḫa du(g)-ga*, 5 Rev. III³ | *6 Rev.
      III¹¹ | [7 Ob. IV³] | *8 Ob. V¹³ | *9 Ob.
      VI⁴ | 10 Ob. VI³ | 11 Ob. V¹¹ | 38 Ob. II⁴
♀ *É-nun-ni*
   sag-dub of *ki-sìg*, 20 Ob. II⁹ | 21 Ob. IV⁵ |
      22 Ob. IV⁷
É-pa-è-dù
   1 Ob. V¹
É-sá-ne-ba-gub
   gin-nita, *40 Ob. I²
É-si-nu
   1 Ob. I³
É-sag-ḫar
   1 Ob. IV⁵

É-šág-ga
  il, 18 Ob. III⁸
E-ta var. E-ta-ě (q. v.)
  1) giš-túg-pi-kar-rá, 9 Rev. I³
  2) over igi-nu-dŭ giš-kin-ti, 24 Ob. I⁷
E-ta-ě
  1) gab-ra-maš, *15 Ob. VIII¹³ | 16 Rev. I⁶ |
    17 Rev. III²⁰ IV¹ (!)
  2) gab-nita×gunu, *15 Ob. VI¹⁹ | 16 Ob.
    VII⁶
  3) giš-túg-pi-kar-rá, 7 Rev. I¹ | 8 Ob. VII⁸ |
    10 Rev. I¹ | *11 Ob. VII⁹ | 12 Ob. VII⁹ |
    13 Ob. VII⁷ | *26 Ob. VI² | [27 Rev. I¹³]
  4) igi-nu-dŭ giš-me, var. giš-kin-ti (q. v.)
    *15 Ob. I¹⁰ | 16 Ob. I¹⁰ | [17 Ob. I¹²]
  5) igi-nu-dŭ giš-kin-ti, 17 Ob. III² | 18
    Ob. I¹⁰
  6) ni-dŭ, [15 Ob. VIII⁵] | 16 Ob. VIII¹⁰ |
    19 Ob. IV³
  7) nu-sar, [33 Rev. III⁸] | 34 Rev. III¹¹
  8) sukkal, 18 Ob. VI⁴
  9) šu-ḫa, *28 Ob. I⁴·
  10) túg-dŭ, 15 Ob. VII¹⁴ | 16 Ob. VIII⁴ |
    17 Rev. II¹⁷ | 18 Ob. IX¹⁰
♀ É-te-me
  ḫar-tud, 17 Ob. VIII² | 18 Ob. VI¹² | *40
    Rev. III¹⁰
É-tud
  1) igi-nu-dŭ giš-me, 15 Ob. I⁷ | *16 Ob.
    I⁷ | [17 Ob. I⁹] | 19 Ob. I⁸
  2) il, 15 Ob. II⁹ | 16 Ob. II¹⁰
  3) nu-sar, 33 Rev. III⁶ | 34 Rev. III⁹ | 35
    Rev. III⁴ | 36 Rev. III⁷
É-ùr
  pa, 44 Ob. II²
É-ùr-bi-dug
  *30 Ob. VI⁴
  si-gìn(?), 17 Rev. III³
En-azag
  1) il, [15 Ob. V²] | *16 Ob. V⁴ | *17 Ob.
    VI³ | 18 Ob. IV¹²
  2) over il, *15 Ob. III¹¹ | 16 Ob. III¹⁰ | *17
    Ob. V⁸ | 18 Ob. IV⁹ | 24 Ob. II⁷
  3) pa-il, 5 Ob. II¹⁵ | *6 Ob. III⁷ | 7 Rev. V²
  4) REC. 344, 7 Rev. III¹⁰ | *38 Rev. I² |
    *40 Rev. I¹⁰
  5) um-mi-a, 33 Rev. I⁶
En-bi
  1) dup-sar, *6 Ob. V⁸ | 7 Rev. I¹⁰ | *8 Rev.

III⁹ | 9 Rev. IV⁴ | *10 Rev. IV⁶ | *11
    Rev. III⁸ | 12 Rev. III¹¹ | 13 Rev. III¹¹ |
    38 Ob. IV⁵
  2) lù-kaš + gar, 46 Ob. III³
En-da-gal-sá
  dup-sar, 17 Ob. VIII¹³ | 18 Ob. VII¹¹
En-gil-sa
  30 Rev. II¹
En-gir-na-sum
  38 Rev. II³
En-ig-gál
  nu-banda, 2 Rev. III³ | 3 Rev. III⁷ | *5 Ob.
    IV⁹ | *6 Ob. V³ | 7 Rev. I⁷, VII¹¹ | 8
    Rev. I*¹⁰, VII² | 9 Rev. II³, VII¹ | 10
    Rev. II⁵, VIII¹ | *11 Rev. I¹⁰, VII³ | 12
    Rev. I¹¹ | 13 Rev. I⁹ | *15 Rev. VIII²
    (Title is omitted but certainly the same
    man) | 16 Rev. VIII¹ | 17 Rev. V*⁸, VIII¹¹ |
    18 Rev. II³ | 19 Rev. IV⁴ | [21 Rev.
    VIII⁷] | *22 Rev. VIII¹¹ | 24 Ob. IV¹⁷ |
    *25 Rev. VI⁴ | *26 Rev. V⁴ | 27 Rev.
    VII¹ | 28 Rev. V¹ | 29 Rev. III⁵ | 30
    Ob. II*³, Rev. IV⁴, VIII² | 31 Ob. II² | 32
    Ob. II⁵ | *33 Ob. II⁷, Rev. VII⁵ | 34 Ob.
    II⁵, Rev. VI¹ | 35 Ob. II³, Rev. V¹⁰ |
    36 Ob. II⁴, Rev. V¹⁰ | 37 Rev. V⁶ | *38
    Ob. IV¹, Rev. V³ | *39 Rev. III³ | 40
    Rev. II*¹¹, VII⁶ | 45 Ob. II² | 46 Rev. I² |
    47 Ob. II² | *49 Rev. I⁴ | 50 Ob. II⁴ |
    51 Rev. I⁶ | 52 Ob. II⁵
ᵈEn-ki-ur-mu
  1) in service of Šaḫ-Bau, 25 Ob. VI¹⁴ |
    *26 Rev. I⁹
  2) simug, *15 Ob. VII⁹ | 16 Ob. VII¹⁵ |
    17 Rev. II¹ | 18 Ob. VIII¹⁴
En-kisal-si
  1) over igi-nu-dŭ giš-me, 15 Ob. II⁴ | 16
    Ob. II⁴ | 17 Ob. II⁵ | *19 Ob. II⁶
  2) nu-sar, 34 Rev. IV¹ | 35 Rev. III¹⁰ |
    36 Rev. III¹³
En-kur-ra-gub-ná
  il, *17 Ob. IV¹² | 18 Ob. III⁵
ᵈEn-lil-bád
  il, 17 Ob. III⁴
ᵈEn-lil-da
  simug, 15 Ob. VII⁸ | 16 Ob. VII¹⁴ | [17
    Rev. I¹⁹]
En-lù-dug
  b. of Lugalalšag, *40 Ob. IV¹⁰

En-na
    dìm, 18 Ob. V⁶ | 24 Ob. II¹⁴
En-na-um-mu
    lù-igi + lagab, 5 Ob. VI² | *6 Ob. VI⁹ |
    7 Rev. III³ | [8 Rev. II¹⁴] | 9 Rev. III⁹ |
    *10 Rev. III¹⁰ | *11 Rev. II¹⁶ | 12 Rev.
    III¹³ | 13 Rev. III¹³ | 38 Ob. V³ | 40
    Rev. I²
En-nanga-rí var. *En-nanga-rí* (q. v.)
    lù-é-nig, 11 Rev. II⁴
En-nanga-rí
    1) *lù-é-nig*, *5 Ob. V¹ | *6 Ob. V¹² | 7 Rev.
    II¹¹ | *8 Rev. II² | 9 Rev. II¹¹ | 10 Rev.
    II¹³ | 12 Rev. II⁶ | 13 Rev. II⁵ | *31 Ob.
    IV¹² | 38 Ob. IV⁷ | 40 Ob. VII¹²
    2) in charge of *sá-dúg é-nig*, *32 Ob. V⁹
En-še-bur(?)-na
    1 Ob. VI³
En-šu-gi-gi
    igi-dub, 12 Rev. VII¹ | *13 Rev. VII² |
    18 Rev. VII⁹ | 23 Rev. X⁹ | 24 Rev. VII¹
En-tum
    1) *gab-ra udu-sìg*, 17 Rev. IV⁸
    2) *lù igi + lagab*, *7 Rev. III⁶ | 8 Rev. III² |
    9·Rev. III¹¹ | *10 Rev. III¹² | 11 Rev. III¹
    3) *mu*, 5 Ob. V⁷ | *6 Ob. VI⁵ | 40 Rev. III²

    4) *sib udu-sìg*, 5 Rev. II⁷ | 6 Rev. II⁷ |
    7 Rev. IV¹¹ | 8 Ob. VI⁷ | 9 Ob. VI¹⁴ |
    *10 Ob. VI¹³ | 11 Ob. VI⁷ | 12 Ob. V¹²
    13 Ob. V¹⁰ | 15 Rev. I² | *16 Rev. I¹⁰ |
    30 Ob. VII¹¹ | 31 Ob. V¹² | *32 Ob. VI⁹ |
    33 Ob. VII⁵ | 34 Ob. VI⁷ | 35 Ob. VI³ |
    36 Ob. VI¹¹
En-túr
    1) *il*, 15 Ob. II¹⁰ | 16 Ob. II¹⁰
    2) *sib ama-gán-ša*, *17 Rev. V⁵
    3) *simug*, 17 Rev. II⁷ | 18 Ob. IX⁴
    4) *šu-ḫa*, *28 Ob. I³
En-ud-da-na
    1) over *gim-ḫar*, 20 Rev. II⁹
    2) *lù-kas + gar*, *6 Ob. IV¹¹
    3) *šu-ḫa*, *28 Ob. II³
En-zi(d)
    edin, 38 Ob. III¹⁰
Erin-ur-mu
    lù igi + lagab, 18 Ob. VII⁵
Eš-kur-gal
    nagar, 40 Ob. V¹⁰
♀ ᵈ*Ezinu-ama-mu*
    gim dun-nig-kú-a, *20 Rev. IV³ | 21 Rev.
    V⁸ | 22 Rev. IV¹⁸

G

♀ *Gà-dú(g)-nam-ḫé-ti*
    1) *gim ḫubur × gig + dìm*, m. of one s.
    and one d., 20 Rev. II¹¹
    2) *ki-sìg* in service of *Gimtarsirsir*, 25 Ob.
    IV¹⁴ | *26 Ob. IV¹¹ | *27 Ob. VI⁷
    3) *sal-an é-gal-la* of *Aenra-mugi*, 25 Rev.
    I¹ | *26 Rev. II¹⁴ | *27 Rev. III¹
    4) under *Urmut*, m. of two ss. and one d.,
    *21 Ob. IX¹⁹
Gà-X
    1 Ob. I¹
♀ *Gà(?)-zi-šág-gal*
    ki-sìg, m. of one s., 21 Ob. VI²⁰
Gab-ra-ni
    1) without title but prob. *sag-engar*, *8 Ob.
    V⁸, [¹⁰] | 9 Ob. V¹³, ¹⁵ | *10 Ob. V¹¹, ¹³ |
    11 Ob. V⁶, *⁸ | 40 Ob. II²
    2) *sag-engar*, *5 Ob. II⁸ | 6 Ob. II⁹, *¹² |
    *7 Ob. V³·[⁶] | 12 Ob. V· ⁴,⁶ | 13 Ob. V³
    3) *sib-udu-sìg*, 5 Rev. II⁶ | *6 Rev. II⁶ |

    7 Rev. IV[¹⁰]· *¹² | *8 Ob. VI⁶· ⁸ | 9 Ob.
    VI¹³· *¹⁵ | *10 Ob. VI¹², ¹⁴ | 11 Ob.
    VI⁶, *⁸ | 12 Ob. V¹¹, ¹⁴, VI³ | 13 Ob.
    V⁹· *¹², VI²
    4) *šub-lugal*, 8 Ob. II⁴ | *9 Ob. II⁶ | *10 Ob.
    II⁶ | 11 Ob. I⁸
Gal . . . .
    1 Ob. VI⁶
Gal-ki-me-ta
    1 Ob. II³
Gala-tur
    1) *il*, 15 Ob. II⁹ | 16 Ob. II⁹ | 17 Ob. IV¹¹ |
    18 Ob. III⁶
    2) *lù Urdam*, 40 Rev. III⁸
    3) *sib ama-gán-ša*, *18 Rev. I¹³ | 24 Ob.
    IV¹² | 37 Ob. *VI⁵, Rev. I¹⁰, III²
    4) over *šu-ḫa*, 28 Rev. II³· ⁴
    5) over *šu-ḫa ab-ba*, 29 Ob. III¹
♀ *Gan-ᵈAn*
    il, 15 Ob. III³ | 16 Ob. III⁴ | *17 Ob. V¹⁵

♀ *Gan-dub*
  ki-sìg in service of *Šaḫ-Bau*, 26 Rev. I²
♀ *Gan-ezen*
  gu-ba of *ki-sìg*, 20 Ob. V³ | *21 Ob. VI⁴
♀ *Gan-ginar-sag*
  ki-sìg, 23 Ob. IX¹⁵
♀ *Gan-ᵈKal*
  1) *ki-sìg*, 23 Ob. III³
  2) *[sag-dub]* of *ki-sìg*, [22 Ob. I¹⁹]
♀ *Gan-ᵈNe-gún*
  ki-sìg, 23 Ob. VII⁴
♀ *Gan-Babbar*
  ki-sìg, 23 Ob. VIII⁹
Geštin-za
  1 Ob. IV⁴, VI⁴
Gi-nim
  1) 30 Rev. I¹¹ | 32 Rev. I⁵
  2) *dù(g)-šagan*, 5 Ob. IV¹³ | *6 Ob. V¹⁰ |
  7 Rev. II¹ | *8 Rev. I¹² | 9 Rev. II⁵ |
  *10 Rev. II⁷ | *11 Rev. I¹² | 12 Rev.
  I¹³ | 13 Rev. I¹¹ | 30 Rev. I¹¹ | 32 Rev.
  I⁵ | 34 Rev. I¹⁰ | 35 Rev. I⁴ | 36 Rev.
  I¹¹ | *40 Ob. VII⁴
♀ *ᵈGid-dū*
  ki-sìg, 23 Ob. VIII⁸
♀ *Gim-ᵈAn*
  il, 18 Ob. IV¹⁵
♀ *Gim-ᵈBa-ú*
  1) d. of *U.*, 25 Ob. IV¹² | *26 Ob. IV⁹ |
  *27 Ob. IV¹⁵
  2) *il*, 17 Ob. IV² | 18 Ob. II¹⁰
  3) *ki-gu*, 23 Rev. II²
♀ *Gim-dù*
  šu-i, 19 Ob. IV¹
♀ *Gim-é-dam*
  1) *ki-sìg*, 23 Ob. VIII⁵
  2) *sag-dub* of *ki-sìg*, 20 Ob. II¹⁰ | 21 Ob.
  IV⁶ | *22 Ob. IV⁸
♀ *Gim-é-zi(d)-da*
  1) *ki-sìg*, 23 Ob. III¹⁷, V⁸, *VI⁸
  2) *sag-dub* of *ki-sìg*, 20 Ob. II⁶ | 21 Ob.
  II¹¹, IV² | 22 Ob. II¹⁴, *IV⁴
♀ *Gim-gannu*
  1) *ki-sìg*, 23 Ob. III¹⁶, V¹⁰
  2) *sag-dub* of *ki-sìg*, 20 Ob. II⁸ | 21 Ob.
  II¹⁰, IV⁴ | 22 Ob. II¹³, IV⁶
♀ *Gim-íd-edin-na*
  il, 17 Ob. III⁹, *¹⁴ | 18 Ob. II⁸
♀ *Gim-nigin*

ki-sìg, 23 Ob. IX¹⁴
♀ *Gim-ᵈNina*
  30 Ob. IV¹⁵ | *35 Ob. V¹³ | 36 Ob. V¹⁵
♀ *Gim-šu-ga-lam-ma*
  nu-gìg, *40 Rev. V⁶
♀ *Gim-šu-il-la*
  ki-sìg, 23 Ob. VIII¹¹
♀ *Gim-tar-sir-sir*
  d. of *U.*, *19 Rev. I⁴ | *25 Ob. VI¹⁰ | *26
  Ob. VI¹⁴ | [27 Rev. II¹³]
Ginar-sag
  il, [15 Ob. III¹²] | 16 Ob. III¹¹
♀ *Gìr-a-ne-ku*
  1) *ki-sìg*, 23 Ob. V⁹
  2) *sag-dub* of *ki-sìg*, 20 Ob. II⁷ | 21 Ob.
  IV³ | 22 Ob. IV⁵
Gìr-ni-ba-ku
  garaš, f. of *Babbar-lù-šág-ga*, 40 Ob. III⁷
Gir-nun, var. *Gir-nun-ki-dug* (q. v.)
  1) title omitted but prob. *gab-rim*, *17 Rev.
  IV¹³ | 19 Ob. V² | 33 Ob. II¹
  2) *gab-rim*, 9 Ob. IV¹ | 10 Ob. III¹² | 11
  Ob. III⁸ | 13 Ob. IV⁸ | 15 Rev. I¹¹ |
  *16 Rev. II⁷ | 30 Ob. I¹¹ | 31 Ob. I¹⁰ |
  [32 Ob. II¹] | 34 Ob. I¹¹ | *35 Ob. I¹⁰ |
  *36 Ob. I¹⁰
Gir-nun-ki-dug
  gab-rim, *7 Ob. III⁹
Gir-su-ki-dug
  šu-ḫa-a dug-ga, *8 Ob. VI³ | 9 Ob. VI¹⁰ |
  *10 Ob. VI⁹ | 11 Ob. VI³
♀ *Giš-ban*
  under *Urnut*, *21 Rev. I⁸
Giš-gig-na-ni-dug
  1) *sag-engar* in service of *Gim-Bau*, *27
  Ob. I⁷
  2) *šu-ḫa*, *28 Ob. III⁵
Giš-[šag-ki-dug]
  from Umma *(Giš-ḫú)ki*, under *Ninipini lù-
  kas + gar*, 20 Ob. VIII⁶
♀ *Gu-bád*
  1) *ki-sìg*, m. of one d., 23 Ob. IV¹⁵
  2) *sag-dub* of *ki-sìg*, 20 Ob. I¹⁵ | 21 Ob.
  III⁸ | *22 Ob. III¹⁰
Gú-en
  šagan-bil, 33 Rev. IV⁶
Gu-ú
  1) *lù šu-gid*, 12 Rev. III⁵ | 13 Rev. III⁵
  2) s. of *Urdam*, '40 Rev. V¹²

Gub-ba-ui
  il, 18 Ob. II[5]
  ni-dŭ, 17 Rev. III[12]

♀ *Gul-ama-mu*
  under *Ninipini lù-kas + gar*, 20 Ob. VII[9] |
  *21 Rev. I[17] | 22 Rev. I[14]

H

♀ *Ḫa-igi*
  1) *gim bar-bi-gál* under *Urmut igi-dub*,
    22 Ob. IX[9]
  2) *ki-sìg*, 21 Ob. VII[6]
Ḫa-ma-ti
  mu, *5 Ob. V[4] | 6 Ob. VI[1] | *7 Rev. II[6] |
  8 Rev. II[4] | 9 Rev. II[13] | 10 Rev. II[15] |

11 Rev. II[6] | 12 Rev. II[10] | 13 Rev. II[9] |
38 Ob. IV[10] | 40 Rev. II[7]
♀ *Ḫa-ti*
  under *Mašdu*, 21 Ob. IX[4]
Ḫu-avnar
  1 Ob. I[2]

I

Ibila-uin-si-sá
  lù igi + lagab, 18 Ob. VII[4]
♀ *Íd-lù* var. *Íd-lù-laḫ-laḫ* (q. v.)
  1) *a-ga-am*, m. of one s. and two dd., 23
    Rev. VI[3]
  2) in service of *Giutarsirsir*, 19 Rev. I[2]
♀ *Íd-lù-laḫ-laḫ*
  a-ga-am, [m. of one d., 20 Rev. II[15]] | m.
  of two dd., 21 Rev. III[21] | m. of one
  son and two dd., *22 Rev. III[17]
Id'-mut
  1) over *edin*, 8 Rev. III[13] | 9 Rev. IV[8] |
    *10 Rev. IV[10] | *11 Rev. III[13]
  2) *sà*, 15 Ob. VII[12] | 16 Ob. VIII[2] | 17
    Rev. II[13]
Igi-ᵈBa-ù-šù
  ni-dŭ, [15 Ob. VIII[8]] | 16 Rev. I[1] | *17
  Rev. III[11] | 18 Rev. I[8]
Igi-bar var. *Igi-bar-lù-ti(l)* (q. v.)
  1) over *ki-sìg*, 21 Ob. VII[13]
  2) *ki-sìg* in service of *Giutarsirsir*, *25
    Ob. V[5] | [26 Ob. V[2]]
  3) in service of *Šaḫ-ᵈBau*, 26 Rev. I[4]
♀ *Igi-bar-lù-ti(l)*
  1) *gù-ba* of *ki-sìg*, 20 Ob. III[1]

2) *ki-sìg*, 23 Ob. V[12]
3) over *ki-sìg*, 22 Ob. VII[1]
4) *sag-dub* of *ki-sìg*, *21 Ob. IV[10] | *22
  Ob. IV[10]
Igi-mu-ᵈŠù-gál
  lù é-nig, *15 Ob. VI[7] | *16 Ob. VI[10] | 17
  Ob. VII[12]
Igi-zi
  šu-ḫa in service of *Gim-Bau*, *26 Ob. III[16] |
  27 Ob. IV[3]
♀ *Igi-ur-kal-ba*
  ki-sìg, 23 Ob. VI[13]
Igi-zi
  1) *šes-sal*, 37 Ob. I[2] | 40 Rev. II[5]
  2) *šu-i*, 12 Rev. II[8] | 13 Rev. II[7] | in ser-
    vice of *Giutarsirsir*, *27 Ob. VI[11]
Il
  1) 40 Ob. V[13]
  2) *ad-ge*, 40 Ob. VI[2]
  3) *dup-sar maḫ*, 40 Ob. III[14]
  4) *šu-ḫa*, 28 Ob. III[7]
Im-ni-pa
  [*udu-uig*]-*kù-[a ba]-laḫ-gi*, 17 Rev. V[11]

K

Ka-gi-na
  30 Rev. II[3]
Ka-ka
  1) *pa*, 49 Ob. I[2]
  2) *sag-eugar*, 12 Ob. V[7] | 13 Ob. V[4]
  3) *šub-lugal*, 7 Ob. I[5, 8] | *8 Ob. II[5] |

9 Ob. II[7] | *10 Ob. II[7] | 11 Ob. I[9] |
12 Ob. V[7]
Ka-ma-ni-zi
  1) title omitted but prob. *šub-lugal*, 6 Ob.
  I[9] | 14 Ob. III[6] | 39 Ob. III[3], Rev. I[4]
  2) *giš-sinig*, *7 Rev. V[9]

3) *nig-en-na*, 40 Ob. IV³

4) *sag-engar*, 12 Ob. V⁵ | 13 Ob. V⁵ | 50 Ob. I²

5) *šub-lugal*, 5 Ob. I⁷ | *7 Ob. II⁷ | *8 Ob. III² | *9 Ob. III⁵ | *10 Ob. III³ | 11 Ob. II¹¹ | 13 Ob. II⁸ | 38 Ob. I⁵ | 40 Ob. IV³

♀ *Ka-šág*

1) *ki-sìg*, 23 Ob. I¹⁶

2) *sag-dub* of *ki-sìg*, *22 Ob. V¹⁰ | m. of one d., 20 Ob. II⁴ | 21 Ob. V⁸

[ᵈ*Kal*]-ga

sag-engar in service of *Gim-Bau*, *27 Ob. I⁹

Ki-bi

over *šu-ḫa*, *28 Ob. III¹

Ki-túg-lù

1) *mu*, *40 Rev. III¹

2) *nagar*, 40 Ob. V¹¹

♀ *Ki-túg-lù*

wife of *Il dupsar maḫ*, 40 Ob III¹³

Kid-gid var. *Lid-kid-gid* (q. v.)

šagan-bil, 33 Rev. III¹¹

Kur-anšu-ni-šu

1) *sã*, *40 Ob. III¹⁶

2) *šu-ḫa*, *28 Ob. I²

L

Lid-kid-gid var. *Kid-gid* (q. v.)

šagan-bil, 34 Rev. IV⁶ | 35 Rev. IV² | 36 Rev. IV⁵

♀ *Lid-ša(g)-gi-na*

sag-dub of *ki-sìg*, m. of one d., 21 Ob. IV¹²

Lù-gid

sib-anšu, 7 Rev. V¹²

Lù-kur-ri-ne·gi

lid + ku, *6 Ob. III⁵ | 7 Ob. V¹¹ | 37 Ob. I⁷, II⁹, III⁷, *IV⁴, V¹, *V¹⁰, Rev. I³, II⁵ | *38 Ob. II⁹

Lù-tu(d)

lid + ku, 5 Ob. II¹²

Lugal-a-mu var.(?) *Lugal-an-mu* (q. v.)

1) *sag-engar* in service of *Gim-Bau*, 25 Ob. I², ³ | 26 Ob. I², *³ | 27 Ob. I², ³

2) *sib-anšu* in service of *Gim-Bau*, *25 Ob. I¹²

3) under *Uu*, 15 Rev. II³ | 16 Rev. II¹⁵ | 17 Rev. V²⁰

Lugal-ab-dug-ga dup-sar, *40 Ob. II³

Lugal-al-šág

1) f. of *Lugaligiannaesu*, *40 Rev. IV¹

2) master of *Lugalanda*, 40 Ob. V²

3) b. of *En-lù-dug*, *40 Ob. IV¹¹

4) *šutug*, 40 Ob. VI¹⁰, Rev. III⁴

Lugal-an-da

1) *patési*, 30 Rev. VII⁵ | 46 Rev. II³ | 51 Ob. II⁶

2) *lù Lugalalšag*, 40 Ob. V¹

Lugal-an-mu var. (?) *Lugal-a-mu* (q. v.)

sib-anšu in service of *Gim-Bau*, *26 Ob. I¹² | 27 Ob. II⁴

Lugal-apin-ni

19 Rev. I⁹

Lugal-bád

lù igi + lagab in service of *Gim-Bau*, *25 Ob. II¹² | *26 Ob. II¹¹ | 27 Ob. III⁴

Lugal-da-nu-me-a

1) *gab-ra udu-sìg*, *17 Rev. IV¹⁰

2) *sib-udu-sig*, 5 Rev. II⁸ | *6 Rev. II⁸ | 7 Rev. IV¹³ | 8 Ob. VI⁹ | *9 Ob. VII¹ | *10 Ob. VII¹ | *11 Ob. VI⁹ | *12 Ob. VI¹ | [13 Ob. V¹³] | 15 Rev. I⁴ | *16 Rev. I¹² | 30 Ob. VII¹⁴ | 31 Ob. VI¹ | 32 Ob. VII¹ | 33 Ob. VII⁸ (!) | *34 Ob. VI¹⁰ | *35 Ob. VI⁵ | 36 Ob. VI¹³

Lugal-é-ni-šu

nu-sar, 35 Rev. III⁶ | 36 Rev. III⁹

Lugal-ᵈEn-lil-li

šu-i in service of *Gim-Bau*, 25 Ob. III¹ | *26 Ob. II¹³ | *27 Ob. III⁶

Lugal-ezen

51 Rev. I⁴

Lugal-gà

ga-šu-dù, 15 Ob. V¹⁷ | 16 Ob. VI² | *17 Ob. VI¹⁸ | 18 Ob. V¹⁰

Lugal-gan

1) *ḫar-tud*, 30 Rev. I⁸

2) *mu*, *18 Ob. V¹⁷

Lugal-geštin

nagar in service of *Gim-Bau*, *25 Ob. I⁷ | *26 Ob. I⁷ | *27 Ob. I¹⁴

Lugal-giš-búr

over *šu-ḫa-a dug-ga*, 5 Rev. III⁵ | *6 Rev. III⁹

Lugal-ia-nun

1) *nim*, *15 Rev. I¹⁶ | 16 Ob. II¹²

2) *udu nig-kú-a ba-laḫ-gi*, 17 Rev. V¹³ | 18 Rev. II⁶

Lugal-igi-an-na-è-su
  s. of *Lugal-alšag*, 40 Rev. III[17]
Lugal-ka-gi-na
  1) *qa-šu-dŭ*, *15 Ob. VI[1] | *16 Ob. VI[4] |
     17 Ob. VII[3]
  2) *šu-ḫa*, *28 Rev. I[1]
Lugal-kês^{ki}
  1) *27 Ob. VI[2]
  2) *lù šuku(-ku) ba* in service of *Gimtar-sirsir*, 27 Ob V[7]
Lugal-kisal-a-gub
  gab-rim, 12 Ob. IV[8]
Lugal-maš-su
  *38 Ob. II[2]
Lugal-me-gal-gal
  šu-ḫa, *28 Rev. III[1]
Lugal-mu var. *Lugal-mu-da-kuš* (q. v.)
  1) *mu*, *5 Ob. V[8] | *38 Ob. V[1] | *40 Rev. I[12]
  2) *sib-anšu-pir-ka*, *8 Ob. III[14] | *9 Ob. IV[4] |
     11 Ob. III[11] | *38 Rev. I[11](?) | 40 Rev. V[14]
Lugal-mu-da-kuš
  1) *mu*, 6 Ob. VI[2] | 7 Rev. II[9] | 8 Rev.
     II[7] | 9 Rev. III[2] | 10 Rev. III[3] | *11 Rev.
     II[9] | 12 Rev. II[13] | 13 Rev. II[12]
  2) *sib-anšu-pir-ka*, 5 Rev. II[2] | *6 Rev. II[2] |
     *7 Rev. V[11] | 10 Ob. IV[2] | 12 Ob. IV[11] |
     13 Ob. IV[11] | 17 Rev. V[2]
Lugal-mu-šú(?)-gál
  over *šu-ḫa*, *28 Rev. II[5]
Lugal-nam-gú-sud
  gab-rim, 33 Ob. II[3] | *34 Ob. II[1]
Lugal-nanga-ra var. *Lugal-nanga-ra-ná* (q. v.)
  1) *gal-úku*, *9 Ob. I[8]
  2) *lù-ḫal*, 8 Ob. I[8]
Lugal-nanga-ra-ná
  1) *a-da-ba*, *15 Rev. II[10] | 16 Rev. III[5]
  2) *gal-úku*, *10 Ob. I[8]
Lugal-nē-tur
  simug, 17 Rev. II[4] | 18 Ob. IX[3]
Lugal-nita-mus
  1) *sib-gud*, 7 Ob. VI[2] | *8 Ob. V[4] | *9 Ob.
     V[9] | 11 Ob. V[2]

  2) *sib-gud-tur-tur*, 10 Ob. V[7] | 37 Ob.
     *II[2, 11], III[9], IV[6], V[3], VI[2], Rev. I[5], II[7]
Lugal-pa-è
  sib-dun, *5 Ob. IV[7] | 6 Ob. V[1] | *7 Rev.
     I[5] | *8 Rev. I[8] | 9 Rev. I[8] | 10 Rev. I[6] |
     11 Rev. I[8] | 12 Ob. I[6] | *13 Ob. I[6] | 14
     Ob. I[6] | 20 Rev. V[2] | 21 Rev. VI[6] | 22
     Rev. VI[1] | 23 Rev.VIII[11] | 24 Rev. II[15] |
     30 Rev. III[9] | *31 Rev. II[1] | 32 Rev. III[7] |
     *33 Rev. III[3] | 34 Rev. III[4] | 35 Rev.
     III[1] | 36 Rev. III[4] | 40 Rev. IV[12]
Lugal-pĭr-ki-ág var. *Lugal-pĭr-ri-ki-ág* (q. v.)
  sukkal, 17 Ob. VII[9]
Lugal-pĭr-ri-ki-ág
  sukkal, *15 Ob. VI[5] | *16 Ob. VI[8] | *18
     Ob. VI[2]
Lugal-sib
  1) over *il*, 15 Ob. IV[14] | *16 Ob. V[1] | 17
     Ob. VI[1] | 18 Ob. V[5] | 24 Ob. II[10]
  2) *pa-il*, 5 Ob. III[1] | *6 Ob. III[8] | 7 Rev. V[3]
Lugal-Lagaš^{ki}
  1) *simug*, 17 Rev. II[5] | [18 Ob. IX[2]]
  2) over *šu-ḫa*, 28 Rev. II[7]
Lugal-ša(g)
  1) *dup-sar*, 17 Ob. VIII[14]
  2) *mu*, 40 Ob. VI[13]
Lugal-ša(g)-lá-tuk
  1) *dup-sar*, 18 Ob. VII[10]
  2) *šu-ḫa*, *28 Ob. III[3], IV[3]
  3) over *šu-ḫa*, *28 Ob. IV[4]
  4) *šu-ḫa ab-ba*, 29 Ob. II[1]
Lugal-šu-maḫ
  1) *mu*, 12 Rev. II[12] | 13 Rev. II[11]
  2) *nagar*, 18 Ob. IX[13]
Lugal-te-da
  in service of *Gimtarsirsir*, 25 Ob. V[14] |
     *26 Ob. V[14] | [27 Rev. I[9]]
Lugal-ur-mu
  1) *lù a-bil*, *15 Ob. VI[10] | *16 Ob. VI[13] |
     17 Ob. VIII[10]
  2) under *gabrim*, *17 Rev. IV[14, 15]

M

Ma-al-ga var. *Ma-al-ga-sug* (q. v.)
  1) *lù igi + lagab*, 40 Rev. I[3]
  2) over *ki-sìg*, 20 Ob. III[13]
  3) *pa ki-sìg*, *5 Ob. IV[2] | *6 Ob. IV[4]

Ma-al-ga-sug
  lù igi + lagab, 7 Rev. III[4]
♀ *Ma-ma-ni*
  sag-dub of *ki-sìg*, 20 Ob. IV[8]

♀ *Ma-ma-tùm*
1) *ki-sìg*, 23 Ob. I¹⁷
2) *sag-dub* of *ki-sìg*, 20 Ob. IV³ | 21 Ob. V¹⁰ | *22 Ob. V¹¹

Maḫ-nam cf. *Nam-maḫ*
1 Ob. VI²

Maš-dū
1) *21 Ob. IX¹⁰ | 25 Ob. VII⁵ | 26 Rev. II⁴
2) *dup-sar*, 20 Ob. VII⁷ | *30 Ob. IV⁴ | *31 Ob. IV⁹ | *32 Ob. V⁴ | 38 Ob. IV³ | *46 Ob. II¹
3) *igi-dub*, 5 Ob. IV⁵ | *6 Ob. IV¹³ | 7 Rev. IV⁵ | 40 Ob. II¹¹

♀ *Maš-gu-la*
ki-sìg, 23 Ob. VI¹²

Maš-na
1 Ob. V⁵

♀ *Maš-tur*
1) *ki-gu*, *23 Rev. I¹³
2) *lù de-ma* of *ki-gu*, 22 Ob. VII¹³

Me-an-ni(?)-si
šeš-sal, 38 Rev. II¹

♀ *Me-kisal* var. *Me-kisal-li* (q. v.)
22 Ob. V¹⁹

♀ *Me-kisal-li*
sag-dub of *ki-sìg*, 20 Ob. IV¹³ | *21 Ob. V¹⁷

Me-lù
pa-il, 7 Rev. V¹

♀ *Me-me*
1) *ki-sìg*, m. of one d., *23 Ob. II³
2) *sag-dub* of *ki-sìg*, m. of one d., *20 Ob. IV¹⁴ | [21 Ob. V¹⁸] | *22 Ob. VI¹
3) *šu-i*, 17 Rev. I² | [18 Ob. VIII¹]

♀ *Me-uigin-ta*
ki-sìg, 23 Ob. IX⁷

Me-pa-nu-sá
lid + ku, 37 Ob. I⁵, II⁷, III⁵, IV⁷, [¹¹], *V⁸, Rev. I¹, II³

ᵈMes-an-du-lù-šá(g)-ga
il, 15 Ob. II¹¹ | 16 Ob. II¹¹ | *17 Ob. IV¹³

Mu-ni
lù-šuku(-ku) ba in service of *Gimtarsirsir*, 27 Ob. V³˒⁴

Mu-ni-da
40 Rev. IV⁵

Mu-ni-urù
mu, 17 Ob. VII⁶

N

♀ *Na-na*
sag-dub of *ki-sìg*, m. of one d., *20 Ob. IV¹

Nam-dam
lid + ku, 37 Ob. I *⁴, II⁶, III⁴, IV⁷˒ [¹⁰], *V⁷, *VI¹⁰, * Rev. II²

♀ *Nam-dam*
gim dun-nig-kú-a, 21 Rev. V¹⁰ | 22 Rev. V⁵ | 23 Rev. VII³

Nam-lù
šagau-bil, 33 Rev. IV² | *34 Rev. IV⁸ | 35 Rev. III¹⁵ | 36 Rev. IV³

Nam-maḫ cf. *Maḫ-nam*
ni-dŭ, 6 Rev. III³ | 15 Ob. VIII³ | *16 Ob. VIII⁸ | [27 Rev. III¹⁰]

Nam maḫ-ni
sukkal, 17 Ob. VII¹⁰ | 18 Ob. VI³

♀ *Nam-niu-au-ua-gam-gam*
ki-sìg in service of *Gimtarsirsir*, 25 Ob. V⁴ | *26 Ob. V¹

♀ *Nam-uru-na-šu* var. *Nam-uru-ni-šu* (q. v.)
under *Amarkišᵏⁱ*, 23 Rev. V¹⁰ | m. of one d., *20 Rev. I³ | *22 Rev. II¹⁴

♀ *Nam-uru-ni-šu*
under *Amarkišᵏⁱ*, m. of one d., 21 Rev. II¹³

Nam . . . . . .
1 Ob. II⁵

♀ *Nam-X(REC. 316)-nu* var. ♀ *Nam-X-mu-ne-dúg* (q. v.)
1) *gim-maš*, m. of one d., 23 Rev. VIII⁶
2) *ni-dŭ*, m. of one d., 17 Rev. III¹⁵

Nam-X(REC. 316)-nu-ne-dúg
túg-dŭ, *15 Ob. VII¹⁵ | *16 Ob. VIII⁵ | 17 Rev. III¹

♀ *Nam-X(REC. 316)-nu-ne-dúg*
1) *ki-sìg*, m. of [one] s. and [one] d., 21 Ob. VI¹⁴
2) *ni-dŭ*, m. of one d., 19 Ob. IV⁵

♀ *Nauga-dim-dug*
under *Ninipini*, *21 Rev. II³ | 22 Rev. II³ | *23 Rev. V¹

♀ *Nauga-ra-šág*
1) *gim dun-nig-kú-a*, 23 Rev. VII⁸
2) *il*, 17 Ob. III¹², IV⁵
3) *ki-gu*, 23 Rev. II¹
4) *lù de-ma* of *ki-gu*, 22 Ob. VII¹⁷

5) *sag-dub* of *ki-sìg*, 21 Ob. II¹⁴ | [23 Ob. IV¹]

Ne-sag
1) [*a*]-*dun Umma (Giš-ḫu)ᵏⁱ*, 20 Rev. IV⁶ | *a-dun-an Umma*ᵏⁱ, 21 Rev. V¹⁴
2) *šu-ḫa*, *28 Ob. II⁵
3) over *šu-ḫa*, 28 Ob. II⁸, Rev. II⁸
4) over *šu-ḫa ab-ba*, 29 Ob. I⁴

Ni-iá-ama-da-rì
1) *il*, 15 Ob. III¹⁵ | 16 Ob. III¹⁴
2) *sib-ama-gán-ša*, 17 Rev. V⁴

Ni-lum-kal
    lù šuku(-ku)ba in service of *Gimtarsirsir*, *27 Ob. V⁶

Ni-ni-pi-ni
1) title omitted, but certainly *lù-kas + gar*, 11 Rev. I² | 21 Rev. II¹⁰
2) *lu-kas + gar*, 5 Ob. III¹¹ | 6 Ob. IV¹⁰ | 7 Rev. IV³ | *8 Ob. VII¹³ | 9 Rev. I¹² | *10 Rev. I¹⁰ | 12 Rev. I⁹ | 13 Rev. I⁷ | 20 Ob. VIII¹³ | *22 Rev. II¹⁰ | 23 Rev. V⁷ | 24 Rev. I¹⁰ | *30 Ob. III⁸ | [31 Ob. III¹⁴] | *32 Ob. IV⁶ | 33 Ob. IV¹⁰ | 34 Ob. IV⁴ | *35 Ob. III¹⁴ | 36 Ob. IV¹ | 38 Rev. I⁴ | 40 Ob. III¹ | 46 Ob. II⁶

♀ *Ni-su-ba*
1) *gim bar-bi-gal* under *Urmut igi-dub*, *22 Ob. IX¹⁰ | 23 Rev. IV¹
2) under *Urmut*, 21 Rev. I⁵

Ni-ti-e
    šu-ḫa, *40 Ob. V⁴

♀ *Nig-banda(-da)*
    il, *17 Ob. VI⁶ | *18 Ob. IV³

Nig-dù-pa-è
1) *lù é-šag-ga*, 17 Ob. VII¹⁵ | 18 Ob. VI⁸
2) *šu-ḫa*, *28 Ob. IV¹

Nig-ga-kur-ra
    ni-dù, 6 Rev. III² | *15 Ob. VIII⁴ | 16 Ob. VIII⁹ | 17 Rev. III⁸

Nig-galu var. *Nig-galu-nu-túm* (q. v.)
    simug(?), 24 Ob. III¹⁹

Nig-galu-nu-túm
1) 17 Rev. II⁹
2) *simug*, 18 Ob. IX⁵
3) *sukkal*, 40 Ob. III⁴

♀ *Nig-ne-šub-bar-ra*
    under *Maš-du*, m. of one s., '21 Ob. IX²

Nigin-mut
1) *sag-engar* in service of *Gimtarsirsir*, 27 Ob. V¹²
2) *sib-udu-sìg*, 5 Rev. II⁵ | 6 Rev. II⁵ | [7 Rev. IV⁹] | *8 Ob. VI⁵ | 9 Ob. VI¹² | 10 Ob. VI¹¹ | 11 Ob. VI⁵ | *12 Ob. V⁹ | 13 Ob. V⁷ | 27 Ob. V¹² | 30 Ob. VII⁸ | *31 Ob. V¹⁰ | *32 Ob. VI⁶ | *33 Ob. VII¹ | 34 Ob. VI⁴ | *35 Ob. VI¹ | *36 Ob. VI⁸

Nimgir-absu
1) *nu-sar*, 34 Rev. IV³ | 35 Rev. III¹² | 36 Rev. III¹⁵
2) over *igi-nu-dù giš-me*, 17 Ob. II⁸, ⁹ | *19 Ob. II⁹, ¹⁰

Nimgir-eš-a-gub
1) *gab-ra dun-ú*, *23 Rev. VII¹⁶
2) *šu-ḫa*, *28 Ob. III⁸

Nimgir-ka-gi-na
1) *nu*, *40 Rev. V⁹
2) *šu-ḫa*, 28 Ob. I⁶

Nimgir-si
    šub-lugal, 7 Ob. I⁶

♀ *Nin-a-gub-ti(l)*
    il, *18 Ob. III¹⁴

♀ *Nin-al-maḫ*
    il, *15 Ob. V⁵ | *16 Ob. V⁷

♀ *Nin-al-šág*
1) *ḫar-tud*, *17 Ob. VIII³ | 18 Ob. VI¹³
2) *ki-sìg*, 23 Ob. IV¹⁷
3) *sag-dub* of *ki-sìg*, *22 Ob. III¹¹ | m. of one d., 20 Ob. I⁸ | 21 Ob. III¹³

♀ *Nin-ama-mu*
1) *ki-sìg* in service of *Gim-Bau*, m. of one d., 25 Ob. II⁴ | [26 Ob. II³] | 27 Ob. II¹⁰

♀ *Nin-ama-na*
1) *ki-sìg*, 23 Ob. II¹²
2) *sag-dub* of *ki-sìg*, 22 Ob. I⁸ | m. of one d., 21 Ob. I⁵

♀ *Nin-azag-zu*
1) *ki-sìg*, 23 Ob. II¹⁴
2) *sag-dub* of *ki-sìg*, m. of two dd., 21 Ob. I¹³ | [22 Ob. I¹⁶]

♀ *Nin-ba-ba*
1) *gim bar-bi-gál* under *Urmut igi-dub*, *22 Rev. I³
2) *gim ḫar*, 20 Rev. II⁴ | 21 Rev. III¹¹

♀ *Nin-bár-da-ri*

1) *il*, *15 Ob. V⁶ | *16 Ob. V⁸ | *17 Ob. VI⁸ | 18 Ob. II¹²

2) *ki-gu*, m. of one d., 20 Ob. V¹¹, *17 | 23 Rev. I *⁷, ¹¹ | m. of two dd., 21 Ob. VII¹⁶, VIII³

3) *lù de-ma* of *ki-gu*, *22 Ob. VII¹⁴

4) *sag-dub* of *ki-gu*, m. of two dd., 22 Ob. VII⁴, ¹⁰

♀ *Nin-bár-gi*

1) *gu-ba* of *ki-sìg*, 20 Ob. II¹³

2) *sag-dub* of *ki-sìg*, 21 Ob. IV⁸ | m. of one s., *22 Ob. IV¹¹

♀ *Nin-da-nu-me-a*

1) *ki-sìg*, 23 Ob. I²⁰, IV¹⁸

2) *sag-dub* of *ki-sìg*, [20 Ob. IV¹⁷] | 21 Ob. III⁹ | 22 Ob. III¹⁴

3) under *Mašdu*, *20 Ob. VII¹

4) under *Urmut*, *21 Ob. IX¹⁵

♀ *Nin-da-nu-me-me (!)*

gim bar-bi-gál under *Urmut igi-dub*, 22 Ob. IX⁶

♀ *Nin-dúg-ga-dú(g)-bi*

1) *ki-sìg* in service of *Gim-Bau*, m. of two ss., 25 Ob. I¹⁴ | *26 Ob. I¹⁴ | 27 Ob. II⁶

2) *ki-sìg* in service of *Gimtarsirsir*, 25 Ob. IV¹³ | *26 Ob. IV¹⁰ | *27 Ob. VI⁵

♀ *Nin-dug-li-sud*

ki-sìg, 23 Rev. II⁸

♀ *Nin-dun-ama-mu*

ki-sìg, 23 Ob. I¹¹

♀ *Nin-é-balag-ni-dug*

1) *gala*, [20 Rev. III¹] | 21 Rev. IV⁵ | 22 Rev. IV⁶ | *23 Rev. VI¹⁵

2) *gim ḫar*, *20 Rev. II¹

3) *ni-du*, 17 Rev. III¹⁷

♀ *Nin-e-dingir-zu*

1) *ki-sìg*, m. of one d., 23 Ob. I¹⁸

2) *sag-dub* of *ki-sìg*, m. of one s. and one d., *22 Ob. V¹²

3) under *Urmut*, m. of two ss., 21 Ob. IX¹⁷

4) under *Uu*, m. of two ss., 15 Rev. II⁴ | 16 Rev. II¹⁶

♀ *Nin-e-ki-ág*

ki-sìg in service of *Gim-Bau*, 25 Ob. II⁶ | *26 Ob. II⁵ | *27 Ob. II¹²

♀ *Nin-é-ninni-šu*

ki-sìg, *23 Ob. VII²⁰

♀ *Nin-é-unug^{ki}-ga-nir-gál*

1) *ki-sìg*, m. of one d., 23 Ob. VIII¹³

2) over *ki-sìg*, *23 Ob. VIII¹⁸ | 24 Ob. VII⁵

3) *sag-dub* of *ki-sìg*, 21 Ob. II¹ | 22 Ob. I¹⁰

♀ *Nin-edin-ni*

1) *gim bar-bi-gál* under *Urmut*, m. of two dd., *22 Ob. IX¹⁴

2) *gim dun-nig-kú-a*, m. of two ss., 23 Rev. VII⁵

3) *il*, 15 Ob. III⁴, *16 Ob. III⁵

4) *ki-gu*, 23 Rev. II¹⁰

5) *ki-sìg*, *23 Ob. VI⁹

♀ *Nin-en-šu-nu-gan-gan*

ni-dŭ, 18 Rev. I¹⁰

♀ *Nin-éš-gu*

1) *gim bar-bi-gál* under *Urmut igi-dub*, 22 Ob. IX³

2) *gim sá-dúg*, 22 Ob. VIII¹⁵ | 23 Rev. III⁸, ⁹

3) under *Mašdu dupsar*, 20 Ob. VI*⁶, ¹⁵ | 21 Ob. VIII¹⁹

4) under *Urmut*, *21 Ob. IX¹²

♀ *Nin-gal-lam*

gim dun-nig-kú-a, m. of three ss., *20 Rev. III¹¹ | 21 Rev. IV¹⁵

♀ *Nin-gan-gál-sud*

ki-sìg, 23 Ob. IX⁹

♀ *Nin-gan-gam*

under *Amarkiš^{ki} lù-kas + gar*, *23 Rev. V¹⁴

♀ *Nin-gil-sa*

il, 17 Ob. III¹¹ | 18 Ob. II⁹

Nin-gìn-zi

ri-ḫu, 38 Ob. II⁶

ᵈ*Nin-gir-su-bád*, var. *Nin-gir-su-bád-mu* (q. v.)

il, 17 Ob. III⁵ | 18 Ob. II³

ᵈ*Nin-gir-su-igi-gub*

1) *gab-ra é-nam*, 17 Rev. IV⁴ | 19 Ob. IV⁹

2) *gab-ra gud*, 15 Rev. I⁶ | 16 Rev. II²

3) *gab-ra gud-tur-tur*, *24 Ob. IV⁹

4) *il*, 15 Ob. II¹² | 16 Ob. II¹² | 17 Ob. IV¹⁴ | 18 Ob. III⁷, ⁹

ᵈ*Nin-gir-su-lù-mu*

1) 20 Rev. II²

2) *lul-an* in service of *Šaḫ-Bau*, 25 Ob. VII³ | *26 Rev. II²

3) *mu*, 17 Ob. VII⁷ | 18 Ob. V¹⁶

4) *qa-šu-dŭ* in service of *Gim-Bau*, 25 Ob. III³ | *26 Ob. II¹⁵ | *27 Ob. III⁸

4*

5) *sukkal,* 5 Ob. V¹² | *6 Ob. VI⁷ | 7 Rev.
    III¹ | 8 Rev. II⁹ | *9 Rev. III⁴ | *10 Rev.
    III⁵ | *11 Rev. II¹¹ | *12 Rev. III¹ | *13
    Rev. III¹ | 38 Ob. V⁸ | 40 Rev. I⁶

ᵈ*Nin-gir-su-men-zi*
   qa-šu-dŭ, 18 Ob. V¹³

ᵈ*Nin-gir-su-ur-mu*
   1) *30 Ob. VI¹³
   2) *il,* 15 Ob. V³ | *16 Ob. V⁵ | *17 Ob. VI⁴
   3) *qa-šu-dŭ,* *18 Ob. V¹¹

♀ *Nin-ḫum-ma-ki-ág*
   gim dun-nig-kú-a, 20 Rev. III⁶ | 21 Rev. IV¹⁰

♀ *Nin-igi-é-an-na-zu*
   gim sá-dúg, 23 Rev. III¹²

♀ *Nin-igi-gá-ur-bi*
   šu-i lù Aennikiág, 19 Rev. I⁵

♀ *Nin-igi-gà-ur-mu*
   šu-i in service of *Aenramugi,* 25 Rev. I¹⁰ |
   *26 Rev. III⁷ | [27 Rev. III¹⁰]

♀ *Nin-igi-gub*
   ki-sìg, 23 Ob. VIII⁴

♀ *Nin-[igi(?)-tab(?)]-me*
   ki-gu, 23 Rev. II⁴

♀ *Nin-igi-tab-mu*
   1) *il,* *15 Ob. IV⁷ | 16 Ob. IV
   2) under *Mašdu dupsar,* *20 Ob. VII⁴
   3) under *Urmut,* *21 Ob. IX¹⁶

♀ *Nin-ka-zi(d)-da*
   1) *ki-sìg,* 22 Ob. IV²² | 23 Ob. V¹⁶
   2) *ki-sìg* in service of *Gimtarsirsir,* 25
    Ob. V¹ | *26 Ob. IV¹² | *27 Ob. VI⁹
   3) over *ki-sìg,* 21 Ob. V⁴ | *22 Ob. V⁶ |
    *23 Ob. VI³ | *24 Ob. VI⁵
   4) *sag-dub* of *ki-sìg,* m. of one s., 21 Ob. IV¹⁶

♀ *Nin-kisal-šu*
   1) *ki-sìg,* 23 Ob. III⁴, IX*¹⁰, ¹¹
   2) *ki-gu,* *23 Rev. II⁵
   3) *sag-dub* of *ki-sìg,* *21 Ob. I¹⁵ | 22 Ob. II¹

♀ *Nin-lù-mu*
   1) *il,* *17 Ob. VI⁷
   2) *ki-sìg,* 23 Ob. I¹⁴
   3) *ki-sìg* in service of *Gim-Bau,* *25 Ob.
    II⁹ | *26 Ob. II⁸ | *27 Ob. III¹
   4) *sag-dub* of *ki-sìg,* *22 Ob. V⁹
   5) under *Amarkiš*ᵏⁱ, 21 Rev. II¹²

♀ *Nin-lù-ti-ti*
   1) *a-ga-am,* [20 Rev. II¹⁷] | m. of one d.,
    21 Rev. IV² | *22 Rev. IV³ | 23 Rev. VI⁹
   2) *gu-ba* of *ki-sìg,* 20 Ob. II¹⁴

♀ *Nin-ma-al-ga-sud*
   1) *gim ḫar* in service of *Gimtarsirsir,*
    *27 Ob. V¹⁵
   2) *ki-sìg* in service of *Gimtarsirsir,* 25
    Ob. V³ | 26 Ob. IV¹⁴

♀ *Nin-ma-tŭm*
   1) *gim sá-dúg,* m. of one d., 22 Ob. VIII¹²
   2) under *Mašdu dupsar,* 20 Ob. VI¹³ |
    m. of one d., *21 Ob. VIII¹⁶

ᵈ*Nin-mar*ᵏⁱ*-ama-dĭm*
   1) *ki-sìg,* 23 Ob. I¹³
   2) *sag-dub* of *ki-sìg,* *20 Ob. IV¹⁶ | 21 Ob.
    V⁶ | *22 Ob. V⁸ | 23 Ob. I¹³

♀ *Nin-maš-e*
   il, *15 Ob. V⁷ | *16 Ob. V⁹ | *17 Ob VI⁹ |
    18 Ob. IV²

♀ *Nin-me-dug-ga*
   ki-sìg, 23 Ob. VI¹⁰

♀ *Nin-mu-da-kus*
   1) *gim bar-bi-gál,* 23 Rev. IV⁵
   2) *gim ḫubur×gŭg + dim,* 21 Rev. III¹⁸ |
    22 Rev. III¹³
   3) *ḫar-tud,* 18 Ob. VII²
   4) *ki-sìg,* 23 Ob. II⁶ | m. of one s., 21 Ob.
    VII³ | 23 Ob. III⁷
   5) *sal é-gal-la,* *26 Ob. V⁸ | 27 Rev. I³
   6) *sag-dub* of *ki-sìg,* 22 Ob. VI⁴
   7) under *Amar-kiš*ᵏⁱ, *20 Rev. I⁷

♀ *Nin-mu-su-da*
   1) *ki-sìg,* 23 Ob. IV¹⁴
   2) *sag-dub* of *ki-sìg,* 22 Ob. III⁹ | m. of
    one d., 20 Ob. I⁶ | 21 Ob III⁶

♀ *Nin-nam-mu-šub-e*
   ki-sìg, *23 Ob. IX¹⁶

♀ *Nin-nig-šu(š)-mu*
   under *Amar-kiš*ᵏⁱ *lù-kas + gar,* *20 Rev. I⁵ |
    21 Rev. II¹⁵ | *22 Rev. II¹⁶ | *23 Rev. V¹¹

♀ *Nin-nir-zi*
   1) *ki-gu,* *23 Rev. I¹⁰ | m. of one d., 20
    Ob. V¹⁵ | 21 Ob. VIII¹
   2) *sag-dub* of *ki-gu,* m. of one d., 22 Ob.
    VII⁸

♀ *Nin-nita-muš*
   ki-sìg, 23 Ob. VIII⁷

♀ *Nin-nu-nam-X (REC. 316).*
   1) *il,* 17 Ob. III¹⁰
   2) *ki-sìg,* *23 Ob. IX¹⁷

♀ *Nin-pad*
   ki-sìg, 23 Ob. VI¹⁴, ¹⁷

♀ *Nin-ra-a-na-gu-lul*
  1) *ki-sig*, m. of one s., 23 Ob. III⁵
  2) *sag-dub* of *ki-sig*, *21 Ob. I¹⁶ | 22 Ob. II²
♀ *Nin-rim-il-il*
  under *Ninipini lù-kas + gar*, 20 Ob. VII¹³ |
    *21 Rev. II² | 22 Rev. II² | 23 Rev. IV¹⁷
♀ *Nin-si-sá*
  ḫar-tud, m. of one s., *17 Ob. VIII⁴
♀ *Nin-sig-ma*
  ki-sig, m. of one s. and one d., 23 Ob. V¹
♀ *Nin-šag-ga*
  ki-sig, *23 Ob. VII³
♀ *Nin-šag-lá-tuk*
  1) *a-ga-am*, m. of two ss. and one d., 23 Rev. VI⁶
  2) *gim dun-nig-kú-a*, m. of two dd., 21
    Rev. V³ | m. of one d., *22 Rev. IV¹⁵
  3) *il*, *17 Ob. III¹³ | 18 Ob. II¹¹
  4) *lù de-ma* of *ki-gu*, 22 Ob. VII¹⁶
♀ *Nin-šes-da*
  il, 15 Ob. III² | 16 Ob. III³
♀ *Nin-šes-ra-ki-ág*
  il, 17 Ob. IV¹⁸ | m. of one d., 18 Ob. III¹²
♀ *Nin-šú-dam-e-ki-ág* var. *Nin-šú-dam-me-ki-ág*
  (q. v.)
  gim dun-nig-kú-a, 23 Rev. VI¹⁷
♀ *Nin-šu-dam-me-ki-ág*
  gim dun-nig-kú-a, 22 Rev. IV⁸ | m. of
    one d., 20 Rev. III³ | 21 Rev. IV⁷
♀ *Nin-šú-gi-gi*
  ki-sig in service of *Gim-Bau*, m. of one d.,
    25 Ob. II² | *26 Ob. II¹ | 27 Ob. II⁸
Nin-šubur¹-ama-mu
  lù é-nig, 17 Ob. VII¹³ | 18 Ob. VI⁶
♀ *Nin-šubur-ama-mu*
  1) *gim sa-dug*, 22 Ob. VIII¹⁶
  2) *il*, *15 Ob. IV⁶ | *16 Ob. IV⁸
  3) *ki-sig*, 21 Ob. VII⁸ | 22 Ob. VI¹⁷
  4) under *Mašdu dupsar*, *20 Ob. VII³ |
    *21 Ob. IX¹
ᵈ*Nin-ti(l)-bád-mu*
  sag-engar, 27 Ob. V¹¹
♀ *Nin-tur*
  1) *ki-gu*, 20 Ob. V¹⁰ | 21 Ob. VII¹⁵ | *23
    Rev. I⁹, II⁷
  2) *sag-dub* of *ki-gu*, 22 Ob. VII³
♀ *Nin-ù-ma*
  1) *gim bar-bi-gál*, 23 Rev. III¹⁶

  2) *gim dun-nig-kú-a*, 20 Rev. III⁵ | 21 Rev.
    IV⁹ | 22 Rev. IV⁹ | [23 Rev. III¹⁸]
  3) *sag-dub* of *ki-sig*, m. of one s. and 1 d.,
    20 Ob. I³ | 21 Ob. III¹⁰ | *22 Ob. III¹⁵
♀ *Nin-um-me-da*
  ki-sig, *21 Ob. VII⁷
♀ *Nin-ur-mu*
  1) *gim bar-bi-gál* under *Urmut*, m. of
    two dd., *22 Rev. I¹
  2) *gim ḫar*, m. of one d., 20 Rev. II⁵ |
    *21 Rev. III⁹
  3) *gim sá-dúg*, 22 Ob. VIII¹¹
  4) *gu-ba* of *ki-sig*, *20 Ob. V² | *21 Ob.
    VI³ | *22 Ob. VI⁶
  5) *il*, *15 Ob. IV⁹ | 16 Ob. IV¹¹ | *17 Ob.
    V¹⁶
  6) *ki-sig*, 23 Ob. I¹²
  7) *sag-dub* of *ki-sig*, 22 Ob. IV¹⁷
  8) under *Mašdu dupsar*, 20 Ob. VI¹³ |
    21 Ob. VIII¹⁵
♀ *Nin-ùr-ni*
  1) *gim dun-nig-kú-a*, 20 Rev. IV⁴ | 21 Rev.
    V⁹ | 22 Rev. IV¹⁹ | 23 Rev. VII⁹
  2) *ki-gu*, *23 Rev. II⁶
  3) *ki-sig*, 23 Ob. VIII¹⁰, IX⁵
♀ *Nin-uru-da-kuš*
  1) *sag-dub* of *ki-sig*, *21 Ob. I¹⁷ | m. of
    one s., *22 Ob. II³
  2) under *Amar-kišᵏⁱ lù-kas + gar*, 21 Rev.
    II¹⁸ | 22 Rev. III³
♀ *Nin-uru-ezen-me-gan-gam-gam*
  under *Ninipini lù-kas + gar*, 20 Ob. VII¹² |
    *21 Rev. II¹ | 22 Rev. II¹ | 23 Rev. IV¹⁶
♀ *Nin-uru-ni-šu-nu-gan-gan*
  il, 17 Ob. III⁸, IV³
♀ *Nin . . . .*
  1) *ki-sig*, *23 Ob. VII¹⁸
  2) *ki-gu*, *23 Rev. I¹⁴
ᵈ*Nina-da-nu-me-a*
  1) over *ki-sig*, *21 Ob. VI¹⁰ | *22 Ob. VI¹² |
    23 Ob. II¹¹ | 24 Ob. VI¹⁰
  2) *pa ki-sig*, *5 Ob. IV³ | *6 Ob. IV⁵ |
    *7 Rev. III¹³ | 8 Ob. VII¹¹ | 9 Rev. I⁶ |
    *10 Rev. I⁴ | 11 Ob. VII¹² | 12 Ob. I⁴ |
    *13 Ob. I⁴ (!) | 14 Ob. I⁴ | *20 Ob. V⁸ |
    40 Ob. II³

---

¹ For this reading see Thureau-Dangin, *Lettres et Contrats*, p. 65.

Nina-ki-dug
  šu-ḫa, *28 Rev. II[1]
^dNina-lù-šág-ga
  il, *17 Ob. V[10]
^dNina-šag-pad
  41 Ob. I[9]
♀ *^dNinni-ama-mu*
  ki-sìg in service of *Gim-Bau*, *25 Ob. II[7] |
  [26 Ob. II[6]] | *27 Ob. II[13]
♀ *^dNinni-da-gal-sá*
  il, 17 Ob. V[14]
♀ *^dNinni-dingir-mu*
  sag-dub of *ki-sìg*, 20 Ob. IV[7] | 21 Ob.
  V[13] | 22 Ob. V[16]
^dNinni-ib-gal
  41 Ob. I[6]
♀ *^dNinni-men-zi-dìm*
  šu-i, 15 Ob. VI[16] | 16 Ob. VII[3]
^dNinni-ur-dìm

il, 15 Ob. III[14] | 16 Ob. III[13] | [17 Ob.
  V[9]] | 18 Ob. IV[10]
Nir-^dDa-gal
  1) *il*, *15 Ob. IV[15] | *16 Ob. V[2] | *17 Ob. IV[15]
  2) *lù è-sag-ga*, [17 Ob. VII[16]] | 18 Ob. VI[9]
♀ *Nita-ni-tum*
  1) *sag-dub* of *ki-sìg*, 20 Ob. IV[9] | 21 Ob.
  V[14] | 22 Ob. V[17] | 23 Ob. II[1]
  2) under *Urmut*, 21 Rev. I[7]
Nita-zi
  qa-šu-du, 5 Ob. V[10] | 7 Rev. II[3] | *8 Rev.
  I[14] | 9 Rev. II[7] | 10 Rev. II[9] | 11 Rev.
  I[14] | 12 Rev. II[2] | *13 Rev. II[1] | 15 Ob.
  V[15] | 16 Ob. V[17] | 25 Ob. VI[15] | *26
  Rev. I[10] | 40 Ob. VII[15]
Numun
  40 Ob. V[7]
♀ *[Nu]-mu-na-sum-mu*
  sag-dub of *ki-sìg*, *21 Ob. I[12]

P

Pu-dug-sag
  1 Ob. I[5]

Q

Qal-si
  1) over *ki-sìg*, 21 Ob. III[4] | *22 Ob. III[7]
  2) *pa ki-sìg*, 7 Rev. III[12] | 8 Ob. VII[10] |
  9 Rev. I[5] | 10 Rev. I[3] | 11 Ob. VII[11] |

  *40 Ob. II[4]
Qum-ku-šu
  sā, 40 Ob. VI[7]

R

♀ *Rig*
  1) *ki-sìg*, 23 Ob. IX[18]
  2) over *ki-sìg*, 23 Rev. I[3] | 24 Ob. VII[8]
  3) *sag-dub* of *ki-sìg*, *20 Ob. I[2] | 21 Ob.
  III[5] | *22 Ob. III[8]

♀ *Rig-ku-šu*
  gim dun-nig-kú-a, 20 Rev. III[7] | 21 Rev.
  IV[11] | m. of two ss. and one d., 22 Rev.
  IV[10] | *23 Rev. VI[19]

S

♀ *Sa-^dSi-ne*
  1) *gim sa-dug*, m. of one s., *22 Ob. VIII[7]
  2) under *Mašdu dupsar*, m. of two ss.,
  20 Ob. VI[9] | m. of one s., 21 Ob. VIII[11]
Sa-tam
  1) 49 Rev. I[1]
  2) *gim-nita*, 5 Rev. III[7] | 6 Ob. II[3] | 38
  Rev. I[6] | *40 Rev. I[14]

  3) *sag-engar* in service of *Gim-Bau*, *25
  Ob. I[9] | *26 Ob. I[9] | *27 Ob. II[2]
Sag-gà-tuk-a
  1) 39 Ob. I[4], Rev. I[2]
  2) title omitted but prob. *sag-engar*, *8 Ob.
  V[9] | *9 Ob. V[14] | 10 Ob. V[12] | *40 Ob. II[1]
  3) *sag-engar*, *5 Ob. II[7] | *6 Ob. II[11] |
  [7 Ob. V[5]]

4) *šu-i-an* in service of *Gimtarsirsir*, *26 Ob.
V¹²

Sag-ginar-ba
1) *šu-ḫa*, *28 Ob. IV⁵
2) over *šu-ḫa ab-ba*, 29 Ob. III³

Sag-mu-eš-tuk
1) *qa-šu-dŭ*, 18 Ob. V¹²
2) *šu-ḫa-a dug-ga*, *11 Ob. V⁷
3) *šu-i-an* in service of *Gimtarsirsir*, *25 Ob.
V¹² | [27 Rev. I⁷]

Sag-ᵈNin-gir-su-da
1) *mu*, *5 Ob. V⁵ | *6 Ob. VI³ | [7 Rev.
II⁷] | 8 Rev. II⁵ | 9 Rev. II¹⁴ | 10 Rev.
III¹ | *38 Ob. IV¹¹ | *40 Rev. II⁸
2) over *il*, 17 Ob. IV¹⁰ | *18 Ob. III⁴ |
24 Ob. II²
3) *pa-il*, *7 Rev. V⁵

♀ *Sal-la*
1) *gim bar-bi-gal* under *Urmut igi-dub*,
m. of one d., *22 Rev. I⁴
2) *gim-ḫar*, m. of one d., 20 Rev. II⁷ | 21
Rev. III¹³

♀? *Sal-si-gál*
*1 Ob. V²

♀ *Sal-šág* var. *Sal-šág-ga* (q. v.)
1) *gim dun-nig-kŭ-a*, 22 Rev. IV¹³ | m. of
one s. and one d., 20 Rev. III⁸ | 21
Rev. IV¹²
2) *ki-sìg*, 23 Ob. II⁵

♀ *Sal-šág-ga*
1) in charge of *sá-dug kas-gig*, *30 Ob.
V¹¹
2) *ki-sìg*, 23 Ob. VII¹⁶

♀ *Si-ma*
ki-sìg, 21 Ob. VII⁵

♀ *Si-pi-tủm*
1) *gim-bar-bi-gál*, *23 Rev. III¹⁷
2) *sag-dub* of *ki-sìg*, 20 Ob. IV⁶ | 21 Ob.
V¹² | *22 Ob. V¹⁵

♀ *Si-um-me*
ki-sìg, *21 Ob. VI¹¹ | 22 Ob. VI¹³ | 23
Ob. I⁸

Sib-ᵈEn-lil-li
qa-šu-dŭ in service of *Gim-Bau*, 25 Ob.
III⁴ | *26 Ob. III¹ | *27 Ob. III⁹

Sib-Lagaš-ki-ág (see var. sqq.)
sā, 16 Ob. VIII¹

Sib-Lagašᵏⁱ-ki-ág (see var. sq.)
sā, 15 Ob. VII¹¹ | 17 Ob. II¹²

Sib-Lagašᵏⁱ-e-ki-ág
sā, 18 Ob. IX⁸

Sib-uru-da-kuš
il, 15 Ob. II¹³ | 16 Ob. II¹³ | 17 Ob. VI² |
18 Ob. II⁶

♀ *Sig-gà-na-gí*
under *Ninipini lù-kas × gar*, 23 Rev. IV¹⁵ |
m. of one s., 20 Ob. VII¹⁰ | m. of two
ss., *21 Rev. I¹⁸ | *22 Rev. I¹⁵

♀ *Sil-tur*
1) *gim bar-bi-gál* under *Urmut igi-dub*,
22 Ob. IX⁵ | *23 Rev. IV⁴
2) *gim-ḫar*, 21 Rev. III¹⁵

Sug-ri-si(g)
ni-dŭ, 18 Rev. I⁷

Ša(g)-gà
1) *gab-nita + gunu*, *5 Ob. VI⁵ | 38 Ob.
V⁶ | *40 Rev. IV¹⁰
2) in service of *Šaḫ-Bau*, *26 Rev. I¹⁵

♀ *Šag-gi-a-gub-ne-dug*
ki-gu, *21 Ob. VIII⁵ | *22 Ob. VIII¹ | *23
Rev. I⁶

Šag-mu-gál
1) *ad-ge*, 18 Rev. I¹
2) *sib ama-gán-ša*, 18 Rev. I¹²

♀ *Ság-šág*
1) wife of *U.*, 2 Rev. II⁴ | *3 Rev. III² |
*7 Rev. VII⁶ | *8 Rev. VI⁵ | 9 Rev. VI⁵ |
*10 Rev. VII⁵ | *11 Rev. VI⁵ | 12 Rev.
VI⁵ | 13 Rev. VI⁵ | 17 Rev. VIII⁶ | 18
Rev. VII⁵ | [21 Rev. VIII¹¹] | 22 Rev.
VIII⁶ | 23 Rev. X⁵ | *24 Rev. VI⁵ | 25
Rev. VI⁹ | *26 Rev. V⁹ | 27 Rev. VI⁴ |
28 Rev. IV⁵ | 29 Rev. III¹ | 33 Rev.
VI⁶ | 34 Rev. V⁵ | 35 Rev. V⁶ | 36 Rev.
V⁶ | *47 Rev. I⁴ | 52 Rev. I³
2) *il*, 18 Ob. IV¹⁶
3) *ki-sìg*, 23 Ob. VII[²]· ⁵ | m. of one s.
and three dd., 23 Ob. IV³
4) over *ki-sìg*, 23 Ob. IV¹³ | 24 Ob. V¹⁸
5) *sag-dub* of *ki-sìg*, m. of five ss. and
2 dd., *21 Ob. I² | m. of three(?) ss.
and three(?) dd., 22 Ob. I²

Šag-tar
lù-šuku(-ku) ba in service of *Gimtarsirsir*,
27 Ob. V¹

♀ *Šag-tar*
gab-ra dun-ú, 22 Rev. V⁷

Šaḫ
  1) *1 Ob. V³ | 17 Rev. II² | 18 Ob. VIII¹⁵ |
    24 Ob. III¹⁶
  2) *ad-ge,* 40 Ob. VI¹
  3) *šu-ḫa,* 28 Rev. III²
  4) over *šu-ḫa,* 28 Rev. III³
  5) over *šu-ḫa ab-ba,* 29 Ob. II⁴
Šaḫ-ᵈBa-u
  s. of *U.,* 25 Ob. VII¹¹ | *26 Rev. II¹¹
♀ *Šes-a-mu*
  gim maš, *20 Rev. IV¹⁵ | 21 Rev. VI⁴ |
  m. of one s., 22 Rev. V¹⁷ | m. of two ss.,
  23 Rev. VIII⁸
♀ *Šes-da* var. *Šes-da-gal-sá* (q. v.)
  sag-dub of *ki-sìg,* 22 Ob. VI³
♀ *Šes-da-gal-sá*
  1) *gim dun-nig-kú-a,* 23 Rev. VII¹⁴
  2) *sag-dub* of *ki-sìg,* *21 Ob. V²⁰
♀ *Šes-da . . . . . ga*
  ki-sìg, *23 Ob. IX¹³
♀ *Šes-ᵈEdin-na*
  1) *gu-ba* of *ki-sìg,* 20 Ob. II¹⁵
  2) *ki-sìg,* m. of one s., 23 Ob. V¹³
  3) *sag-dub* of *ki-sìg,* *21 Ob. IV⁹ | m. of
  one s., 22 Ob. IV¹³
♀ *Šes-e-a-na-ag*
  1) *ki-gu,* m. of two ss., *20 Ob. V¹³ | *21
  Ob. VII¹⁸
  2) *ki-sìg,* m. of two ss. and one d., 23 Ob.
  VII⁷
  3) over *ki-sìg,* *23 Ob. VII¹⁴ | *24 Ob. VII¹
  4) *sag-dub* of *ki-gu,* m. of two ss., 22 Ob. VII⁶
Šes(?)-ki-na
  pa, *1 Ob. IV²
Šes-ki-ne-šub-na
  šu-ḫa, *28 Ob. II¹¹
Šes-kur-ra
  mu, 5 Ob. V⁶ | *6 Ob. VI⁴ | 7 Rev. II⁸ |

  8 Rev. II⁶ | 9 Rev. III¹ | *10 Rev. III² |
  *11 Rev. II⁸ | 12 Rev. II¹¹ | 13 Rev. II¹⁰ |
  *38 Ob. IV¹² | *40 Rev. II⁹
Šes-lù-dug
  1) *dup-sar,* [15 Ob. VI¹²] | 16 Ob. VI¹⁵ |
  17 Ob. VIII¹⁵
  2) *qa-šu-dù* in service of *Gimtarsirsir,* *26
  Ob. V⁶ | 27 Rev. I¹
  3) *sag-engar* in service of *Gimtarsirsir,*
  27 Ob. V¹⁰
  4) *šub-lugal,* 5 Ob. I³ | 7 Ob. II³ | *8 Ob.
  II¹¹ | 9 Ob. II¹¹ | *10 Ob. II¹¹ | *11 Ob.
  II⁴ | 13 Ob. II⁶ | *38 Ob. I³
  5) title omitted, but prob. *šub-lugal,* 6 Ob.
  I³ | 12 Ob. II⁶ | 14 Ob. III³ | 40 Ob.
  IV²
Šes-sá(g)-ga
  lù-kas + gar, 31 Rev. II⁵
Šes-tur
  1) *lù igi + lagab,* 5 Ob. VI³ | *6 Ob. VI¹⁰ |
  *7 Rev. III⁵ | 8 Rev. III¹ | 9 Rev. III¹⁰ |
  10 Rev. III¹¹ | 11 Rev. II¹⁷ | 12 Rev.
  III¹⁴ | 13 Rev. III¹⁴ | 38 Ob. V⁴ | 40
  Rev. I⁴
  2) *šu-ḫa,* *28 Ob. II⁹
♀ *Šes-ur-mu*
  gu-ba of *ki-sìg,* 20 Ob. III²
Šu-na var.(?) *Šu-na-mu-gi* (q. v.)
  il, [15 Ob. V¹] | 16 Ob. V³ | *17 Ob. III⁶
Šu-na-mu-gi
  il, 18 Ob. II²
Šu- 𒐊
  sinnug, 17 Rev. II⁶ | 18 Ob. IX²
Šu-tur-ga-ti
  qa-šu-dù in service of *Šaḫ-Bau,* 25 Ob.
  VI¹² | *26 Rev. I⁷

                       T

Tur-sib
  gal-úkn, 9 Ob. I¹⁰

                       U

Ú-da
  šu-ḫa, 28 Ob. II¹⁰
Ú-ne-ni
  1) 13 Rev. I³

  2) *igi-dub,* 10 Rev. II²
Ú-túm
  1) *giš-tũg-pi-kar-rá,* 40 Ob. II⁷, III¹⁹
  2) *šu-ḫa-a dug-ga,* *7 Ob. IV⁵ | *8 Ob

V¹⁶ | 9 Ob. VI⁷ | 10 Ob. VI⁶ | *11 Ob.
V¹⁴

Ú-ú

1) *15 Rev. II⁷ | 16 Rev. III² | 17 Rev. I⁵ |
*33 Rev. I⁹

2) *dup-sar,* *6 Ob. V⁷ | 17 Ob. VIII¹² |
18 Ob. VII⁹

3) *gal-úku,* 9 Ob. I⁹

4) *igi-dub,* 30 Rev. I⁵ | 31 Ob. VII² | 32
Ob. VII⁹

5) in service of *Aenramugi,* 25 Rev. I¹² |
26 Rev. III⁹ | [27 Rev. III¹²]

6) in service of *Gim-Bau,* 25 Ob. IV¹ |
*26 Ob. III¹⁴

7) REC. 344, 17 Rev. V¹⁸ | 18 Rev. II¹¹ |
24 Ob. V⁵ | *33 Rev. I³ | 34 Rev. I⁷ |
35 Rev. I¹ | 36 Rev. I⁸ | 37 Rev. I⁸,
III⁴

8) *sangu é-gal,* 17 Rev. VI¹ | 34 Rev. I¹⁵ |
35 Rev. I⁹ | 36 Rev. I¹⁶ | among the
giš-kin-ti (!), *9 Ob. V³ | *10 Ob. V² |
11 Ob. IV¹²

9) *šub-lugal,* *7 Ob. I¹⁰

♀ *Ú-ú*

ki-sìg, 21 Ob. VI¹² | *22 Ob. VI¹⁴

Uḫ-ki

1 Ob. I⁴

Um-um

sã, 40 Rev. IV¹⁴

Ur-ᵈAb-ú

1) *giš-túg-pi-kar-rá,* *12 Ob. VII⁶ | 13 Ob.
VII⁴

2) over *igi-nu-du,* 18 Ob. I⁸ | 19 Ob. III⁶ |
*24 Ob. I⁵

3) *sag-engar,* *40 Rev. IV⁸

Ur-. . . . . ga

šu-ḫa, *28 Ob. I⁷

♀ *Ur-azag-gi*

ki-sìg, 23 Ob. VI¹⁶

Ur-ᵈBa-ú

1) *mu,* *15 Ob. VI³ | *16 Ob. VI⁶ | 17 Ob.
VII⁵ | 18 Ob. V¹⁵

2) *nagar,* 17 Rev. II¹⁵ | 18 Ob. IX¹²

3) REC. 344, 37 Ob. VI⁷ | 47 Ob. I⁴

Ur-dù

1) *gal-úku,* 9 Ob. I⁷ | *10 Ob. I⁷

2) *lù-ḫal,* *8 Ob. I⁷

3) *ni-dù,* *5 Ob. VI⁷ | 6 Ob. VII¹ | 7 Rev.

III⁸ | 8 Rev. II¹¹ | 9 Rev. III⁶ | 10 Rev.
III⁷ | *11 Rev. II¹³ | 12 Rev. III³ | 13
Rev. III³ | *38 Ob. V¹⁰ | 40 Rev. I⁸

4) *qa-šu-dù,* 15 Ob. V¹⁶ | 16 Ob. VI¹ |
17 Ob. VI¹⁷ | 18 Ob. V⁹

5) *saḫar,* 40 Ob. I⁶

Ur-dam

1) 38 Ob. II¹

2) *engar,* 40 Ob. IV⁶, Rev. IV*²

3) f. of *Gu-ú,* 40 Rev. V¹³

4) *lù šú-gid,* *8 Rev. III⁶ | 9 Rev. IV¹ |
*10 Rev. IV³ | 11 Rev. III⁵

5) master of *Galatur,* 40 Rev. III⁹

Ur-ᵈDumu-zi

sib-gud, 5 Ob. II¹⁰ | 6 Ob. III² | *7 Ob.
VI¹ | 8 Ob. V⁵ | 9 Ob. V¹⁰ | *10 Ob.
V⁸ | 11 Ob. V³ | 37 Ob. II³, III¹, *¹⁰, IV⁷,
V⁴, VI¹, Rev. I⁶, II⁸ | *38 Ob. III¹

Ur-dun var. *Ur-ᵈDun-pa-è* (q. v.)

1) *giš-tug-pi-kar-rá,* *6 Ob. IV² | *8 Ob.
VII³ | 9 Ob. VII¹² | 10 Ob. VII⁹ | 11
Ob. VII³ | 12 Ob. VII³ | 13 Ob. VII¹ |
*15 Ob. II⁷ | 16 Ob. II⁷ | 38 Ob. III¹² |
*40 Rev. III¹⁴

2) over *igi-nu-dù,* 17 Ob. II¹² | 18 Ob. I⁶ |
*19 Ob. III⁴ | 24 Ob. I³

Ur-ᵈDun-pa-è

giš-tú-pi-kar-rá, *7 Ob. VII⁴

Ur-é-ninni

1) *dam-kàr,* 40 Ob. I⁹

2) *gal dam-kàr,* 52 Ob. II¹

Ur-ᵈEn-ki

1) 39 Ob. I², III⁵

2) *gal-úku,* 9 Ob. I⁵ | *10 Ob. I⁵

3) *lù-ḫal,* 8 Ob. I⁵

4) *nagar,* *40 Ob. VI⁴

5) over *šu-ḫa,* 28 Ob. III⁶

6) *sag-engar,* 5 Ob. II⁶ | 6 Ob. II¹⁰ | *7
Ob. V⁴

7) *sib-gud,* 15 Rev. I⁸ | *16 Rev. II⁴

Ur-ᵈEš-ir-nun

lul, *15 Rev. II¹² | 16 Rev. III⁷

[*Ur-gà]-da*

sag-engar in service of *Gim-Bau,* *27
Ob. I⁸

Ur-ᵈGašam

il, *15 Ob. III¹⁷ | *16 Ob. IV² | *17 Ob.
V¹¹

Ur-ginar-sag
   1) *lù-kas + gar*, 5 Ob. III[12]
   2) *šu-ḫa-a dug-ga*, *7 Ob. IV[6] | [8 Ob. VI[1]] | 9 Ob. VI[8] | 10 Ob. VI[7] | 11 Ob. VI[1]

Ur-ka-si
   šu-ḫa, *28 Rev. I[4]

Ur-ki
   1) *gab-rim* (?), 17 Rev. IV[17]
   2) *ni-dŭ*, [15 Ob. VIII[6]] | 16 Ob. VIII[11] | 17 Rev. III[9]
   3) *nu-sar*, 34 Rev. III[13] | 35 Rev. III[8] | 36 Rev. III[11]
   4) over *igi-nu-dŭ*, 15 Ob. II[1] | *16 Ob. II[1] | 17 Ob. II[2] | 19 Ob. II[3]
   5) *šu-ḫa*, 28 Rev. II[2]

Ur-mut
   1) title omitted, but prob. *igi-dub*, 11 Rev. I[1] | 21 Rev. I[1]
   2) 7 Rev. IV[6] | 8 Rev. I[5] | 9 Rev. I[14] | 10 Rev. II[1] | 12 Rev. I[3] | [13 Rev. I[1]] | 22 Rev. I[12] | 24 Rev. I[6] | *25 Ob. III[12] | *26 Ob. III[9] | 27 Ob. III[17] | 33 Ob. VI[7] | 34 Ob. V[14] | 35 Ob. V[15] | 36 Ob. V[17]
   3) *igi-dub* over *gim bar-bi-gal*, 23 Rev. IV[13]
   4) *sangu nig*, 51 Ob. II[2]

Ur-ni
   lù a-bil, *15 Ob. VI[9] | 16 Ob. VI[12] | *17 Ob. VIII[9] | 18 Ob. VII[7]

Ur-nigin
   šu-ḫa, 28 Ob. III[4]

Ur-dNin-dar
   1) *nagar*, 40 Ob. V[9]
   2) *šu-ḫa*, 28 Rev. II[6]

Ur-dNin-gir-su-da
   mu, *11 Rev. II[7]

Ur-dNin-meš
   šu-ḫa, 28 Ob. II[4]

Ur-dNin-muš ✕ muš-da-ru
   1) *pa-il*, *5 Ob. III[2] | 6 Ob. III[9] | 7 Rev. V[4]
   2) over *il*, *15 Ob. V[13] | 16 Ob. V[15] | 17 Ob. VI[15] | *24 Ob. II[13]

Ur-dNin-sar
   1) *gìn-nita*, 5 Rev. III[8] | *6 Ob. II[4] | *38 Rev. I[7] | *40 Rev. II[1]
   2) *lù-zig-ga*, 8 Rev. III[4] | 9 Rev. III[13] | *10 Rev. IV[1] | 11 Rev. III[3] | 12 Rev. III[7] | 13 Rev. III[7]

   3) *šub-lugal*, 7 Ob. II[9]

Ur-dNinni
   1) *má-láḫ*, 15 Rev. II[8] | 16 Rev. III[3] | 17 Rev. VI[4] | 18 Rev. II[14] | 24 Ob. V[8]
   2) *ni-dŭ*, 18 Rev. I[6]

Ur-dPa-giš-gibil-sag
   1) *ni-dŭ*, 15 Ob. VIII[9] | *16 Rev. I[2]
   2) *simug*, 17 Rev. II[8]

Ur-sag
   1) title omitted, but prob. *šub-lugal*, *6 Ob. I[10] | 12 Ob. I[10], [11] | 14 Ob. II[3, 5]
   2) *gal-úku*, 8 Ob. I[10] | 9 Ob. I[12] | 10 Ob. I[10]
   3) over *gal-úku*, *8 Ob. I[13] | 9 Ob. II[1] | *10 Ob. II[1]
   4) *qa-šu-dŭ* in service of *Šah-dBau*, 25 Ob. VI[11] | *26 Rev. I[6]
   5) *šub-lugal*, 5 Ob. I[8] | 7 Ob. II[8] | 11 Ob. I[3] | 13 Ob. I*[9], II[1] | 38 Ob. I[6]

Ur-še-da-lum-ma
   il, *18 Ob. II[1]

Ur-šu-dam
   udu nig-kú-a ba-laḫ-gi, *17 Rev. V[7] | 18 Rev. II[2]

Ur-dŠu-nir-da
   1) title omitted, but prob. *šub-lugal*, 12 Ob. II[3] | 14 Ob. II[8]
   2) *šub-lugal*, *7 Ob. I[3] | 8 Ob. II[1] | *9 Ob. II[3] | [10 Ob. II[3]] | *11 Ob. I[5] | 13 Ob. II[4]

Ur-ur
   lù šuku(-ku) ba in service of *Gimtarsirsir*, 27 Ob. V[2]

♀ *Uru-é-nu-mu-si*
   ki-sìg, 23 Ob. VI[11]

Uru-ka-gi-na
   1) *lugal*, 2 Rev. II[5] | 3 Rev. III[3] | 4 Rev. I[1] | *7 Rev. VII[7] | *8 Rev. VI[6] | 9 Rev. VI[6] | *10 Rev. VII[6] | 11 Rev. VI[6] | *12 Rev. VI[6] | 13 Rev. VI[6] | 17 Rev. VIII[7] | 18 Rev. VII[6] | *21 Rev. VIII[12] | 22 Rev. VIII[7] | 23 Rev. X[6] | 24 Rev. VI[6] | 25 Rev. VII[1] | *26 Rev. V[10] | 27 Rev. VI[5] | *28 Rev. IV[6] | 29 Rev. III[2] | 32 Rev. VI[5] | 33 Rev. VI[7] | 34 Rev. V[6] | 35 Rev. V[7] | 36 Rev. V[7] | 39 Rev. III[6] | 40 Rev. VII[9] | 41 Rev. V[5] | 47 Rev. I[5] | 52 Rev. I[4]

2) *pa-te-si*, 5 Rev. VI[3] | 6 Rev. VI[5] | 15 Rev. VII[5] | [16 Rev. VII[6]] | 20 Rev. VII[5] | *31 Rev. V[5]

Uru-ka-gi-na-dEn-lil-zu

1) *lù A + en-ra-gin*, *43 Ob. I[1]
2) [*lù A + en-ra-mu-gi*], (cf. 25 Rev. II[5] | 26 Rev. III[14]), *27 Rev. IV[1]

Uru-ka-gi-na-dNin-gir-su-ge-zu

1) *lù A + en-ra-gin*, *43 Ob. I[2]

2) [*lù A + en-ra-mu-gi*], *27 Rev. IV[2]

Uru-ka-gi-na-dNina-zu

1) *lù A + en-ra-gin*, *43 Ob. II[1]
2) [*lù A + en-ra-mu-gi*], *27 Rev. IV[3]

♀ *Uru-na-a-na-gu-lul*

1) *ki-sìg*, *23 Ob. III[18]
2) *sag-dub* of *ki-sìg*, 21 Ob. II[12] | 22 Ob. II[15]

Z

♀ *Za-na*

1) *gim bar-bi-gál* under *Urmut igi-dub*, 22 Ob. IX[7]
2) *gim dun-nig-kú-a*, *20 Rev. IV[2] | *21 Rev. V[5] | 22 Rev. IV[17] | 23 Rev. VII[7]
3) *il*, *15 Ob. III[5, 6] | *16 Ob. III[6] | 17 Ob. V[2]
4) *ki-sìg*, 23 Ob. II[13]
5) *sag-dub* of *ki-sìg*, 21 Ob. V[11](!) | 22 Ob. I[9]
6) *udu nig-kú-a ba-lah-gi*, 17 Rev. V[15] | 18 Rev. II[8]
7) under *Amar-kiš*[ki], 20 Rev. I[1] | 21 Rev. II[11] | 22 Rev. II[11] | 23 Rev. V[8]
8) under *Ninipini lù-kas × gar*, [20 Ob. VIII[1]]
9) under *Mašdu*, *21 Ob. IX[5]
10) under *Uu*, 15 Rev. II[6] | 16 Rev. III[1]

♀ *Zabar(-bar)-tur*

over *ki-gu*, 23 Rev. II[12] | 24 Ob. VII[15]

Zag-mu

1) *gal-ùku*, 9 Ob. I[6] | *10 Ob. I[6]
2) *lù-hal*, 8 Ob. I[6]
3) *sib-anšu*, 5 Rev. II[3] | *6 Rev. II[3] | [8 Ob. III[13]] | * 9 Ob. IV[3] | *10 Ob. IV[1] | 11 Ob. III[10] | 12 Ob. IV[10] | 13 Ob. IV[10] | *38 Rev. I[9] | *40 Rev. III[12]
4) *šagan-kiš*, *8 Ob. IV[8] | *9 Ob. IV[13] | *10 Ob. IV[11] | 11 Ob. IV[3]

Zar-la

*1 Ob. VI[1]

♀ *Zi-la-la*

1) *gim bar-bi-gál* under *Urmut*, *22 Ob. IX[2] | m. of one d., 23 Rev. III[14]
2) under *Mašdu dupsar*, *20 Ob. VI[7]
3) under *Urmut*, *21 Ob. IX[11]

♀ *Zi-li*

1) *gim bar-bi-gál* under *Urmut igi-dub*, 22 Ob. IX[8]
2) under *Amar-kiš*[ki] *lù kas × gar*, *20 Rev. I[6] | m. of one d., 21 Rev. II[16] | 22 Rev. III[1] | *23 Rev. V[12]
3) under *Urmut*, 21 Rev. I[3, 10]

♀ *Zi-mu*

1) *il*, 17 Ob. IV[16]
2) *ki-sìg* in service of *Gim-Bau*, *25 Ob. II[8] | *26 Ob. II[7] | 27 Ob. II[14]

Zi-mu-dDa-gal

1) *il*, 15 Ob. II[14] | *16 Ob. III[1]
2) *ni-dù*, [15 Ob. VIII[7]] | 16 Ob. VIII[12]

♀ *Zi-na*

1) *ki-sìg*, m. of one d., 23 Ob. I[4]
2) *sag-dub* of *ki-sìg*, m. of one d., 22 Ob. IV[15]

♀ *Zi-zi*

1) *sag-dub* of *ki-sìg*, m. of one s. and one d., *20 Ob. II[1] | m. of two dd., *21 Ob. III[20]

X(REC. Supp. 5 ter)-gig-mu

1 Ob. II[4]

X(ibid.)-kúr

1 Ob. IV[1]

X(ibid.)-li

1 Ob. III[5]

X(ibid.)-nu-me

1 Ob. IV[6]

X(ibid.)-sag-má

1 Ob. II[1]

X(REC. 186)
    in service of *Gimtarsirsir*, 25 Ob. VI[3] |
    [26 Ob. VI[7]] | ²27 Rev. II[3]
X(REC. Supp. 339 bis)
    gab-ra udu-nig-ku-a, 5 Rev. II[10] | 6 Rev.

II[10] | [7 Rev. IV[15]] | 8 Rev. III[14] | 9 Rev.
IV[9] | 10 Rev. IV[11] | 11 Rev. III[14] | 12
Ob. VI[5] | 13 Ob. VI[4]
X-mi-du
    I Ob. III[1]

. . . . . . *ama(?)* . . . .
    gim bar-bi-gal under *Urmut*, 23 Rev. IV[2]
. . . . . . *ama . . . tùr(?)*
    šu-ḫa, 28 Ob. III[2]
. . . .(?) . . *ba . . .*
    I Ob. V[6]
d. . . . . *dá*
    I Ob. VII[4]
♀ . . . . *dim (?) . . . en (?)*
    under *Ninipini*, 20 Ob. VIII[2]
. . . . .(?) . . . *dim*
    I Ob. III[4]
. . . . *gal (?)*
    šu-ḫa, 28 Ob. I[1]
♀ . . . . *lu* . . . . *X (REC. 316)-sud*

ki-sìg, 23 Ob. VI[6]
. . . . *m[a]* . . .
    gim sá-du(g), m. of one d., 23 Rev. III[6]
. . . . *nam + gunu?*
    I Ob. VII[1]
. . . . . . *nin (?)* . . . . .
    šu-ḫa, 28 Ob. III[9]
d. . . . . . *nun (?) . . . da*
    I Ob. VII[2]
♀ . . . . . *ta (?)-pad-[d]a*
    ki-sìg, 23 Ob. VI[7]
. . . . *ta* . . . .
    I Ob. VII[3]
♀ . . . . *u . . . dingir-mu (?)*
    gim bar-bi-gal-la, 23 Rev. IV[3]

TEXTS

Plate 1

No. 1

Obverse

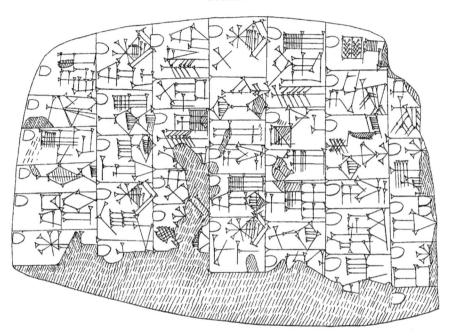

No. 2

Obverse   Reverse

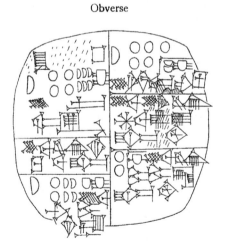 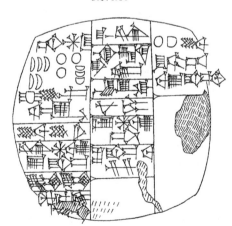

Plate 2

No. 3

Obverse   Reverse

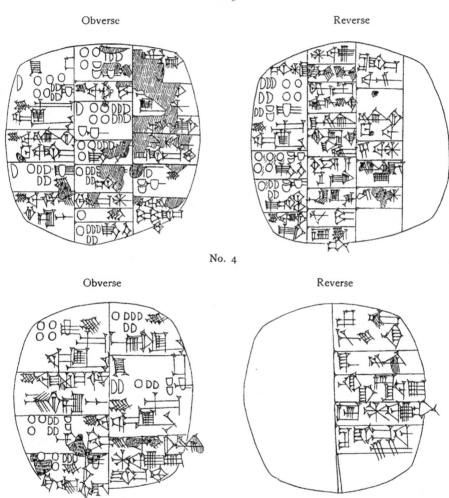

No. 4

Obverse   Reverse

Plate 3

No. 5

Obverse

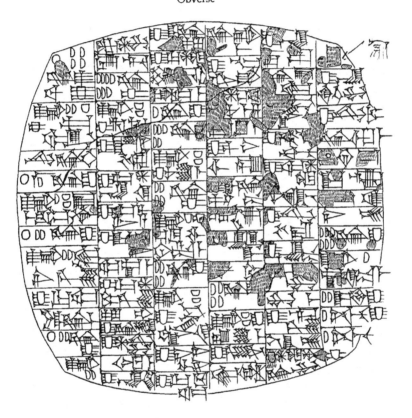

Plate 4

No. 5

Reverse

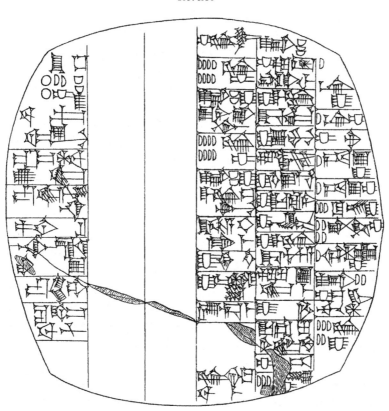

Plate 5

No. 6

Obverse

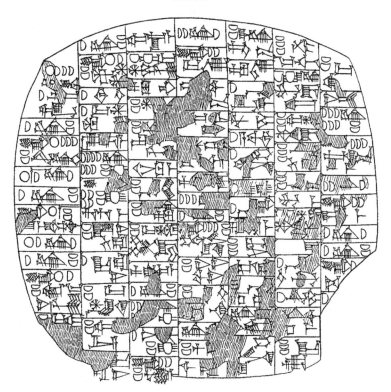

Plate 6

No. 6

Reverse

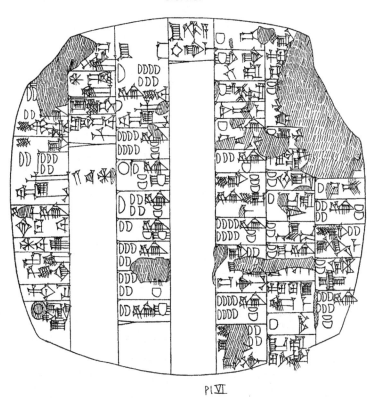

Pl VI

Plate 7

No. 7

Obverse

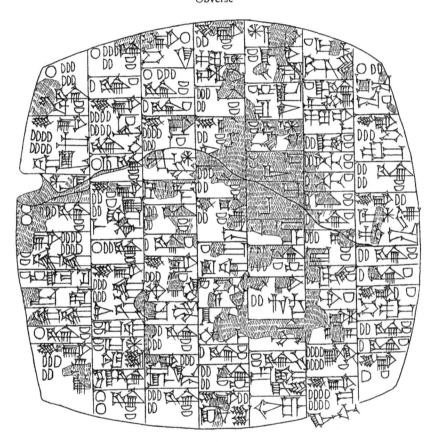

Plate 8

No. 7

Reverse

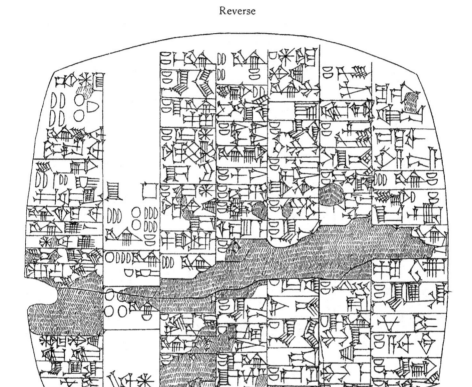

Plate 9

No. 8

Obverse

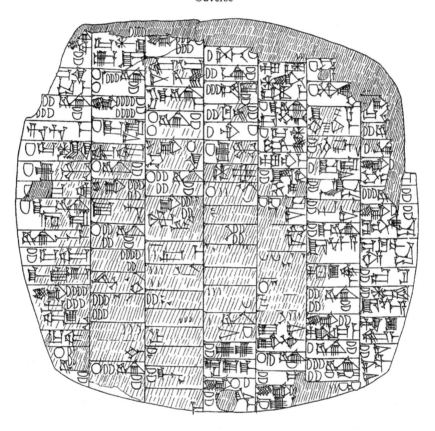

Plate 10

No. 8

Reverse

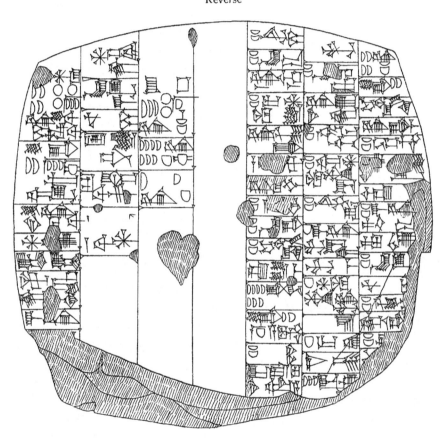

Plate 11

No. 9

Obverse

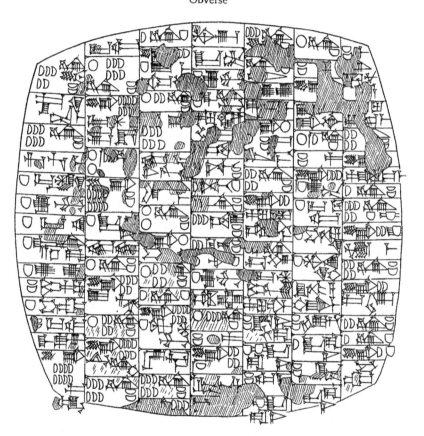

Plate 12

No. 9

Reverse

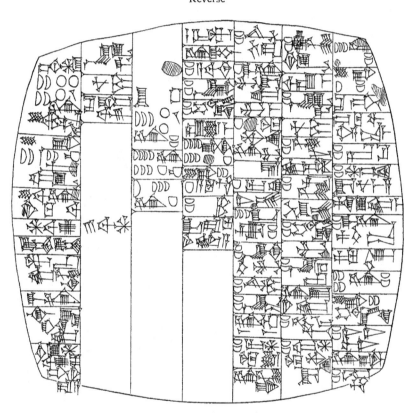

Plate 13

No. 10

Obverse

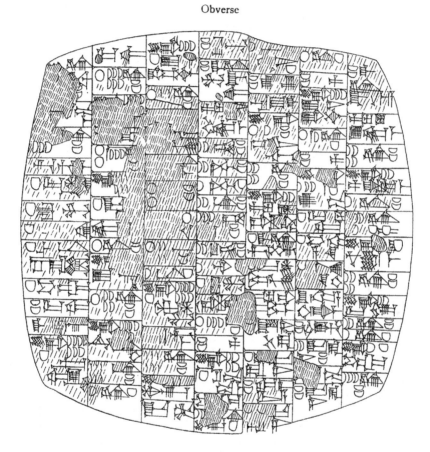

Plate 14

No. 10

Reverse

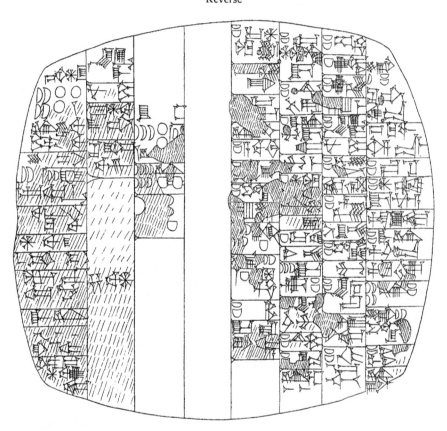

Plate 15

No. 11

Obverse

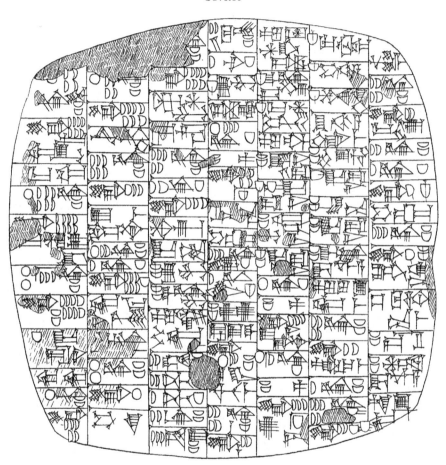

Plate 16

No. 11

Reverse

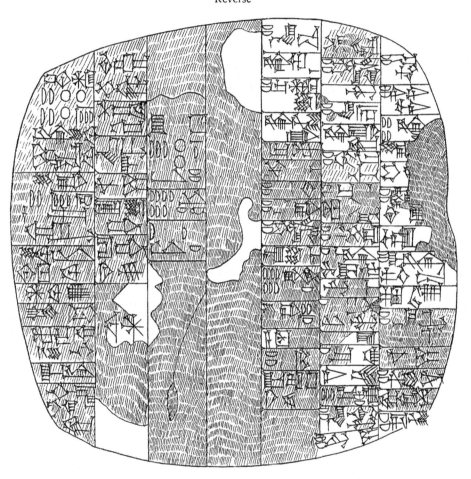

Plate 17

No. 12

Obverse

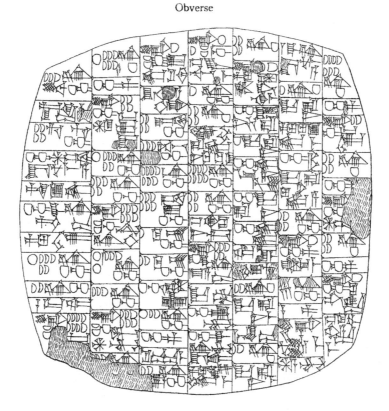

Plate 18

No. 12

Reverse

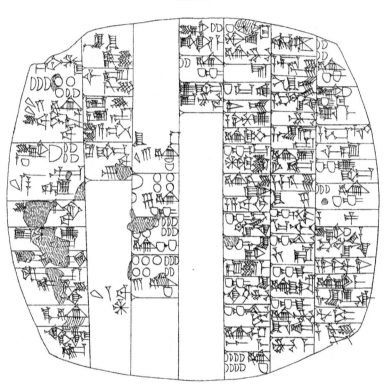

Plate 19

No. 13

Obverse

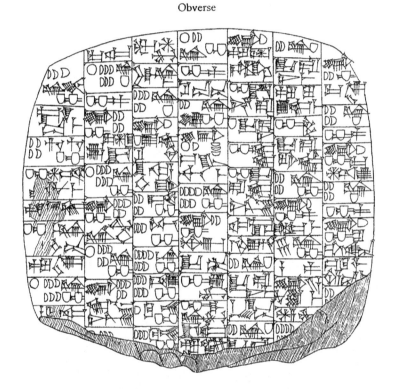

Plate 20

No. 13

Reverse

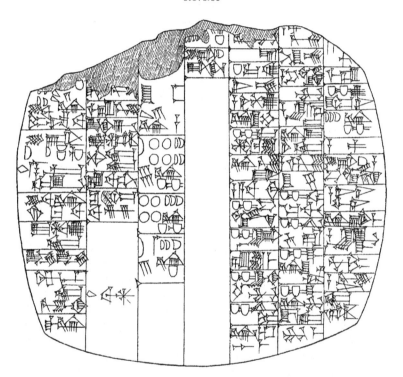

Plate 21

Obverse

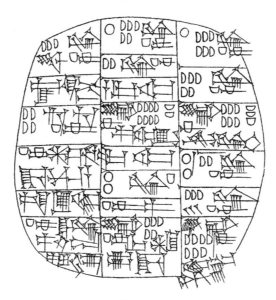

Reverse

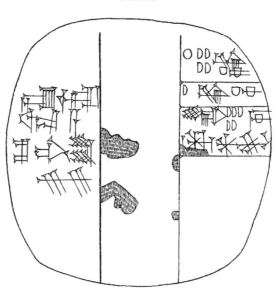

Plate 22

No. 15

Obverse

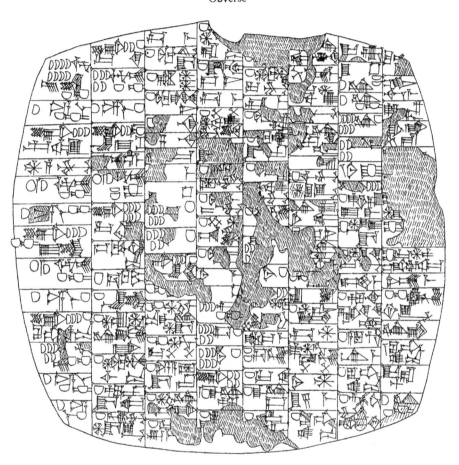

Plate 23

No. 15

Reverse

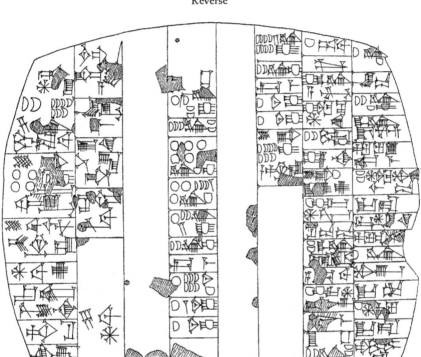

Plate 24

No. 16

Obverse.

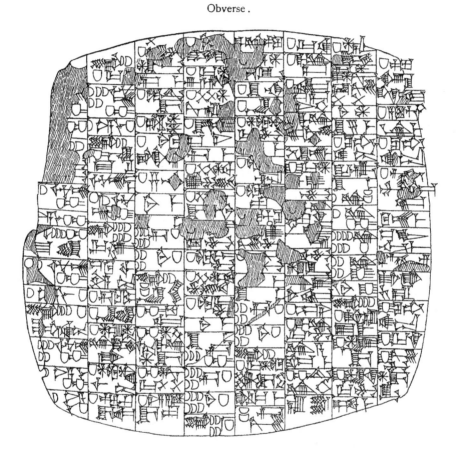

Plate 25

No. 16

Reverse

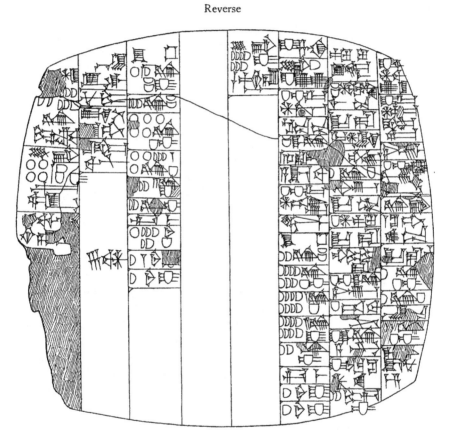

Plate 26

No. 17

Obverse

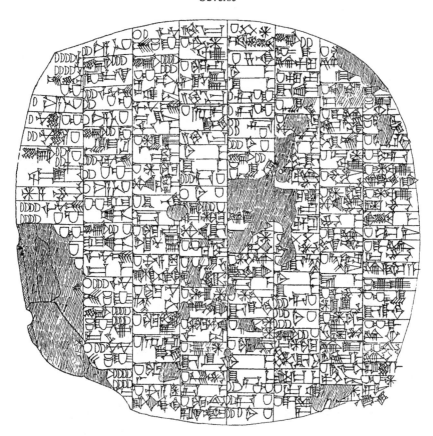

Plate 27

No. 17

Reverse

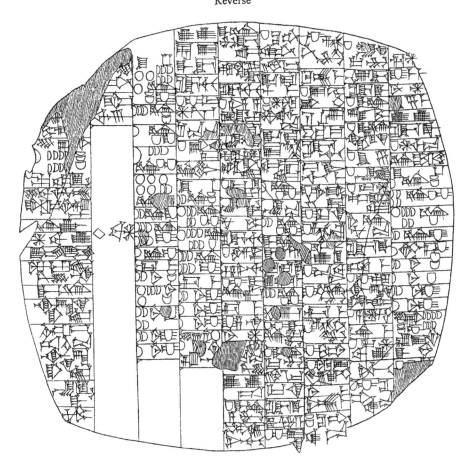

Plate 28

No. 18

Obverse

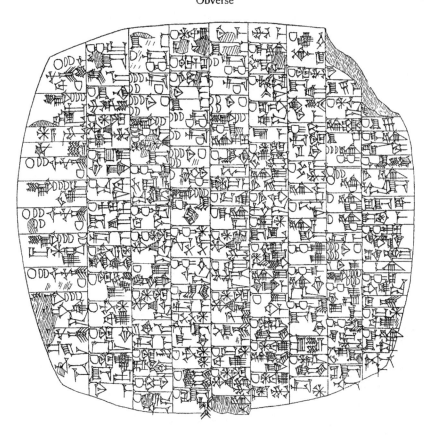

Plate 29

No. 18

Reverse

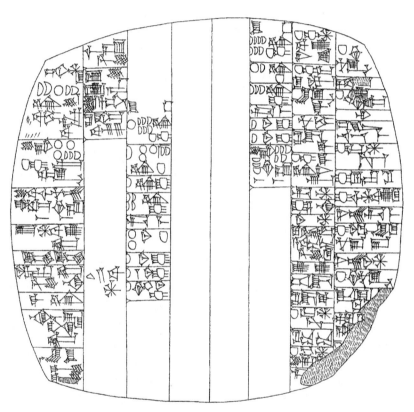

Plate 30

No. 19

Obverse

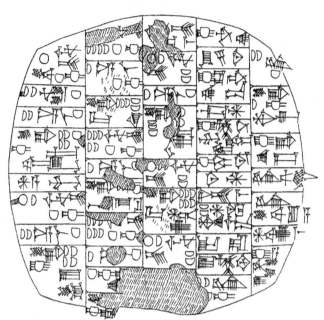

Reverse

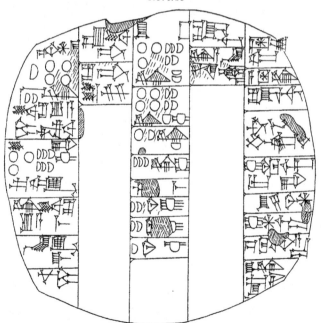

Plate 31

No. 20

Obverse

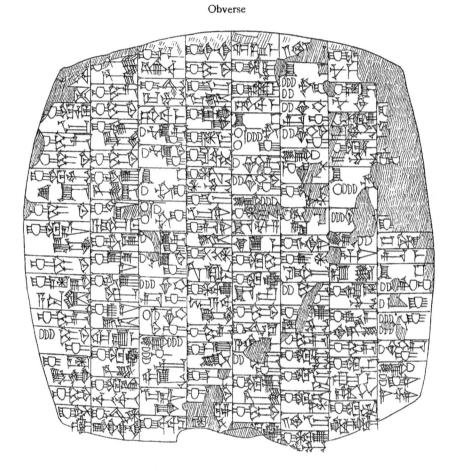

Plate 32

No. 20

Reverse

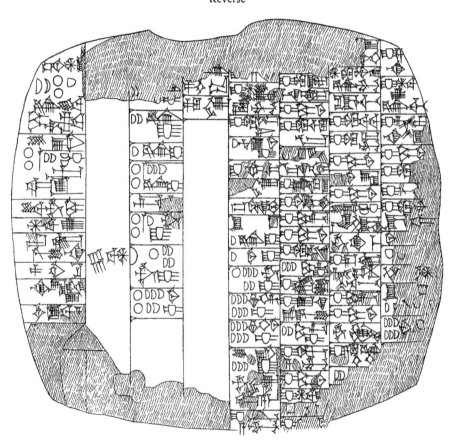

Plate 33

No. 21

Obverse

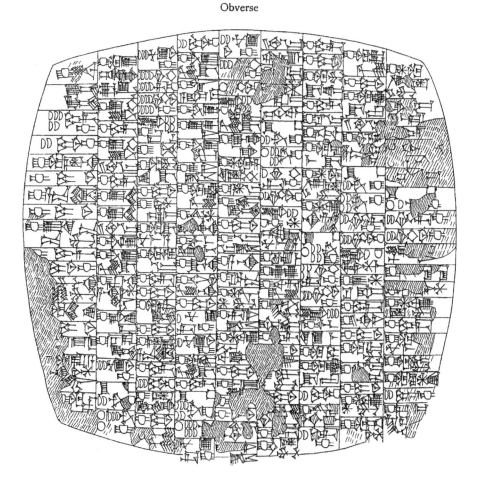

Plate 34

No. 21

Reverse

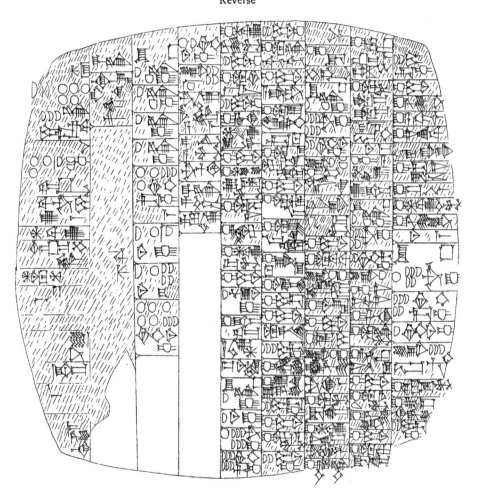

Plate 35

No. 22

Obverse

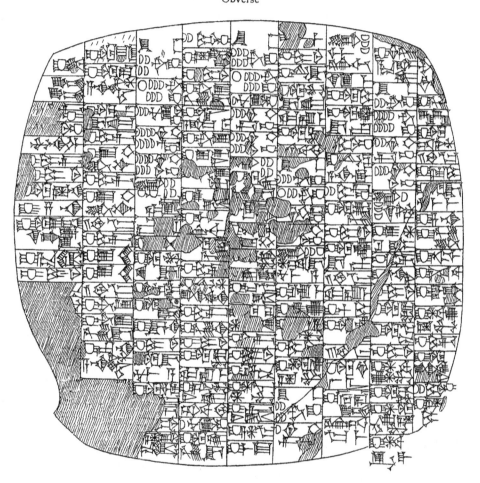

Plate 36

No. 22

Reverse

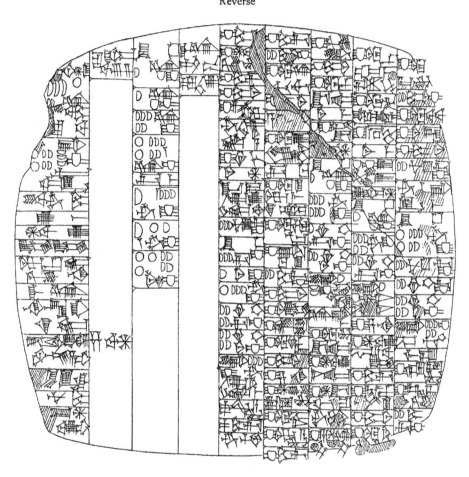

Plate 37

No. 23

Obverse

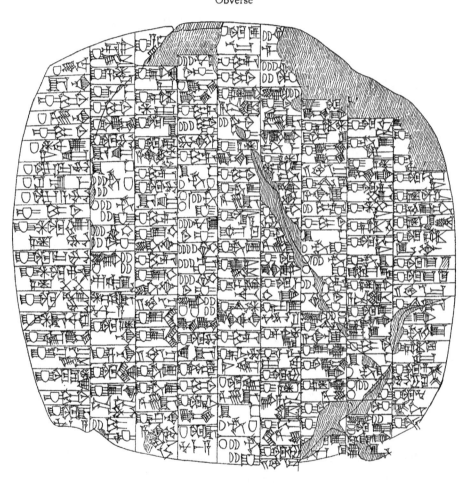

Plate 38

No. 23

Reverse

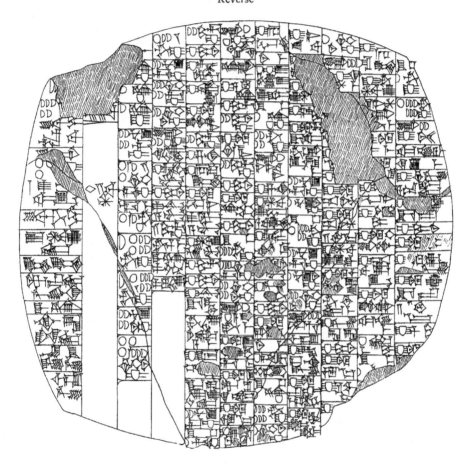

Plate 39

No. 24

Obverse

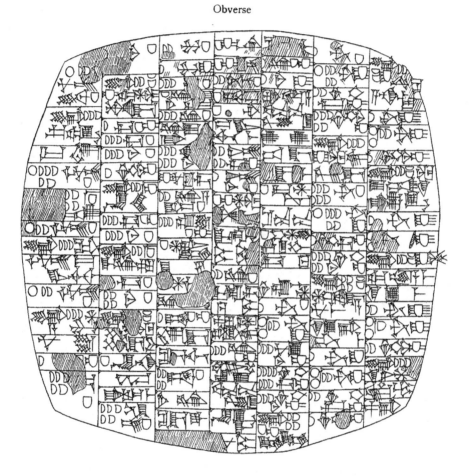

Plate 40

No. 24

Reverse

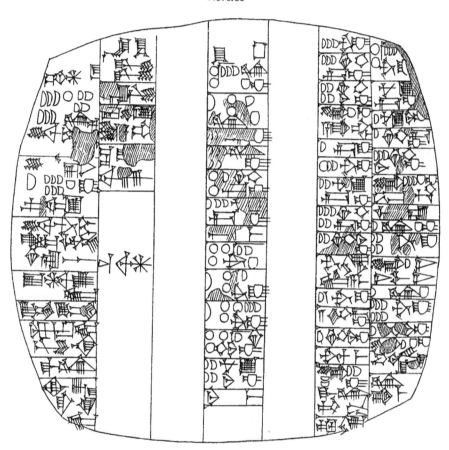

Plate 41

No. 25

Obverse

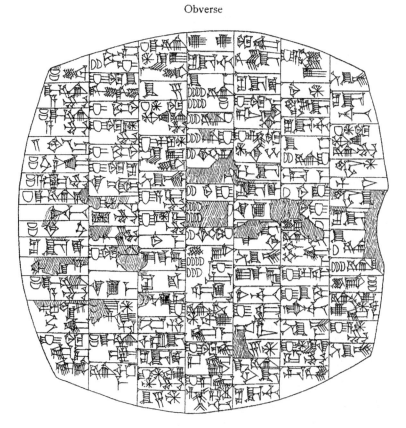

Plate 42

No. 25

Reverse

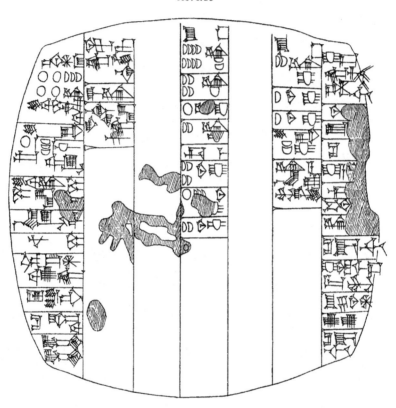

Plate 43

No. 26

Obverse

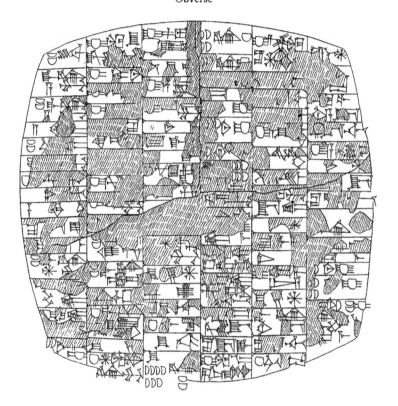

Plate 44

No. 26

Reverse

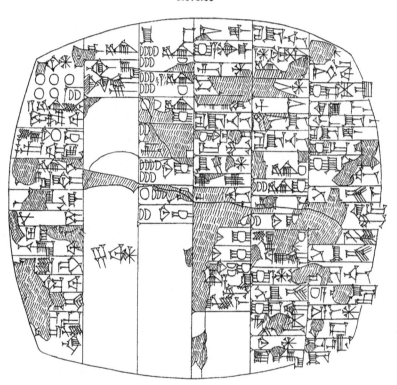

Plate 45

No. 27

Obverse

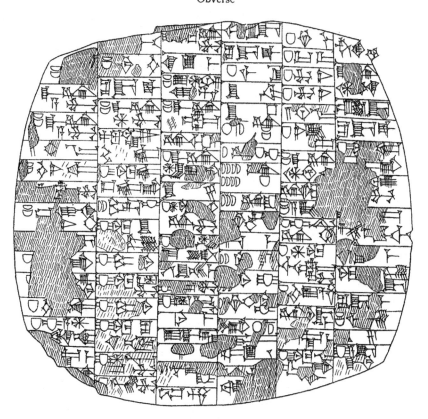

Plate 46

No. 27

Reverse

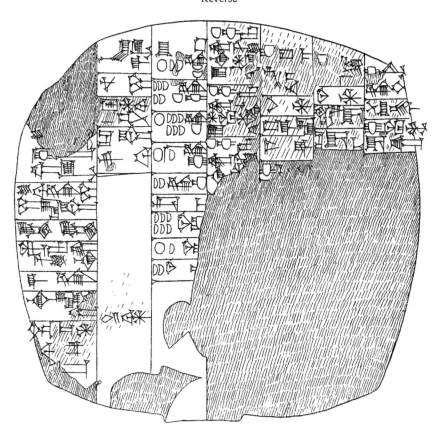

Plate 47

No. 28

Obverse

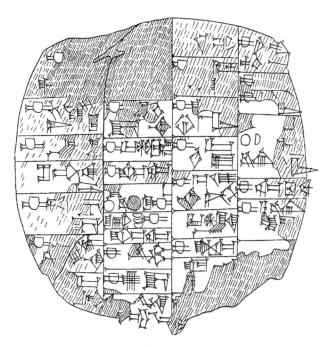

No. 29

Obverse

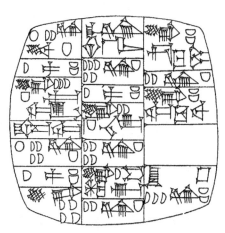

Plate 48

No. 28

Reverse

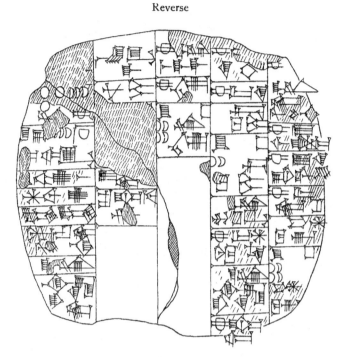

No. 29

Reverse

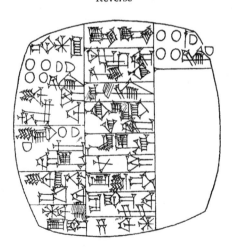

Plate 49

No. 30

Obverse

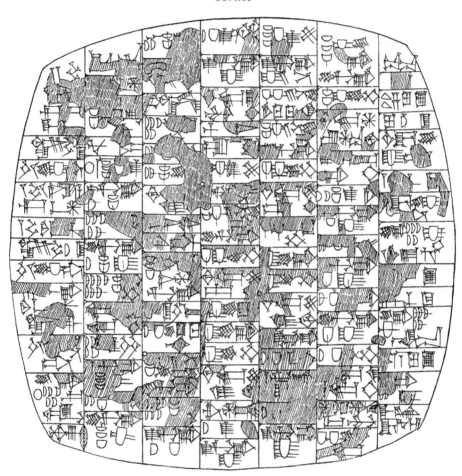

Plate 50

No. 30

Reverse

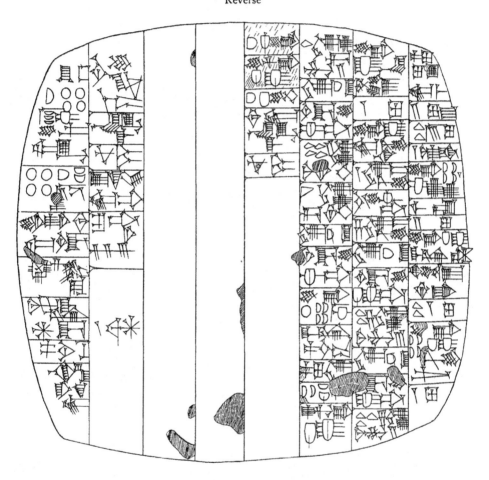

Plate 51

No. 31

Obverse

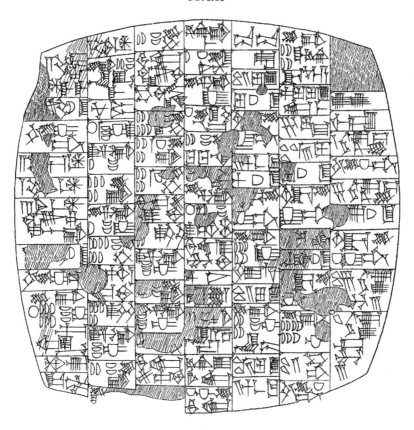

Plate 52

No. 31

Reverse

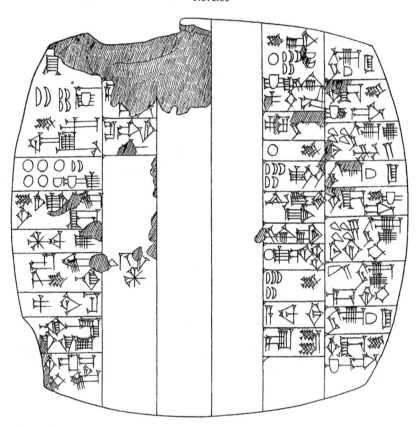

Plate 53

No. 32

Obverse

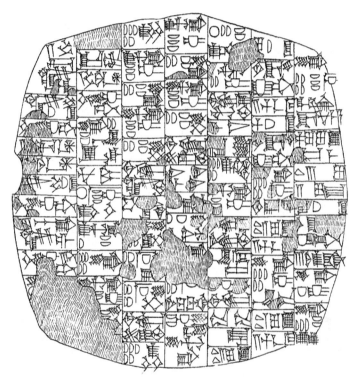

Plate 54

No. 32

Reverse

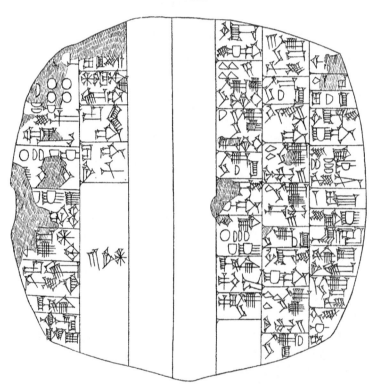

Plate 55

No. 33

Obverse

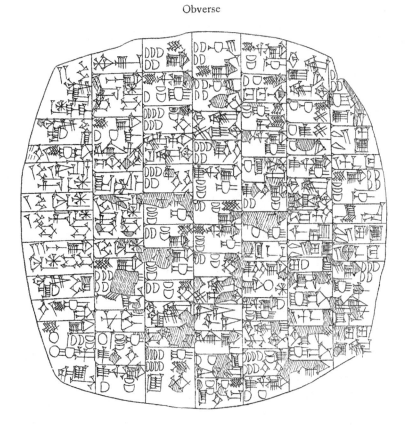

Plate 56

No. 33

Reverse

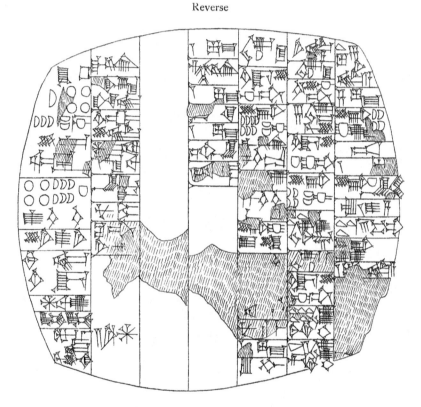

Plate 57

No. 34

Obverse

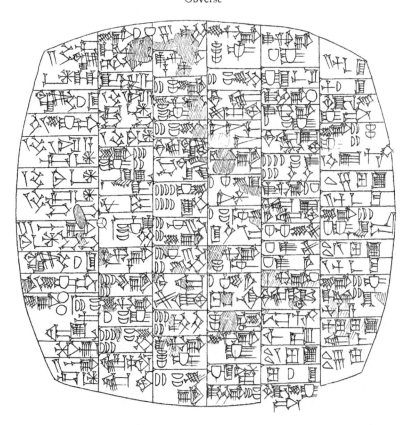

Plate 58

No. 34

Reverse

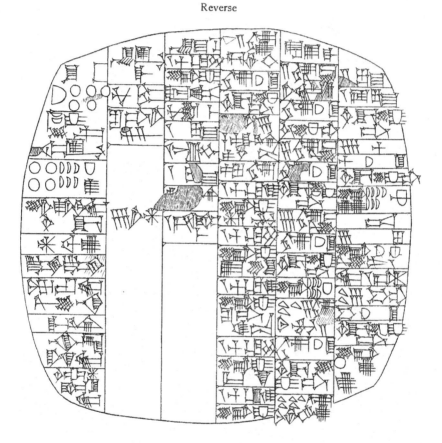

Plate 59

No. 35

Obverse

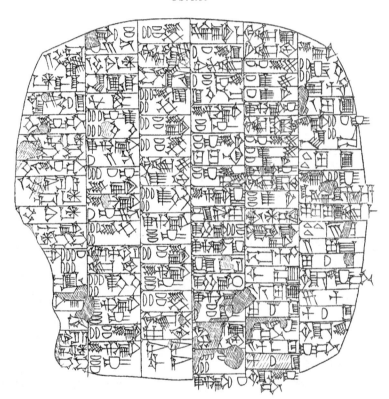

Plate 60

No. 35

Reverse

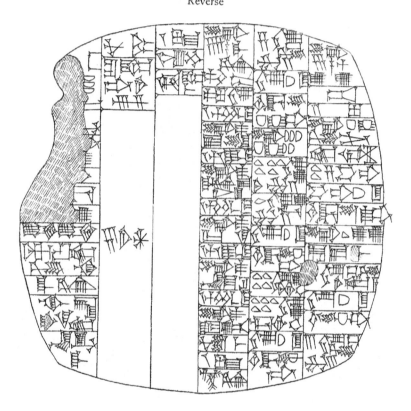

Plate 61

No. 36

Obverse

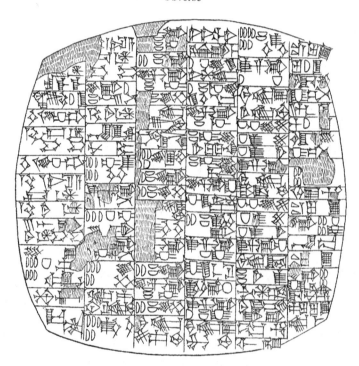

Plate 62

No. 36

Reverse

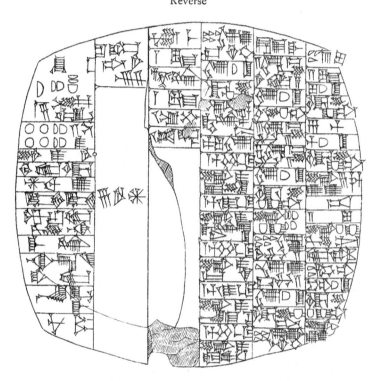

Plate 63

No. 37

Obverse

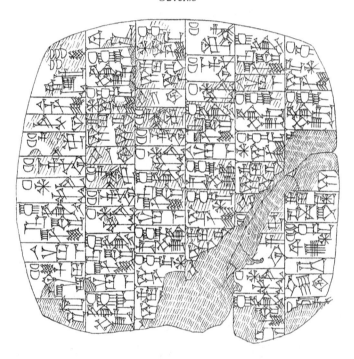

Plate 64

No. 37

Reverse

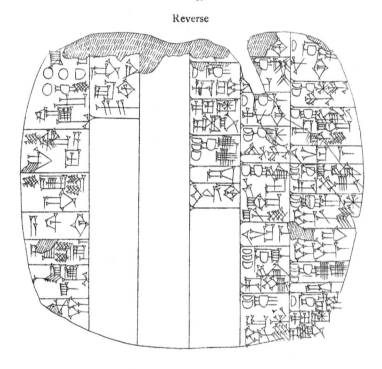

Plate 65

No. 38

Obverse

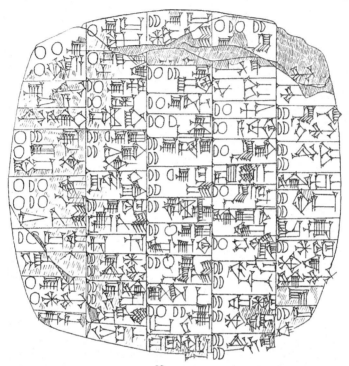

No. 39

Obverse

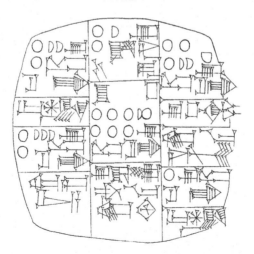

Plate 66

No. 38

Reverse

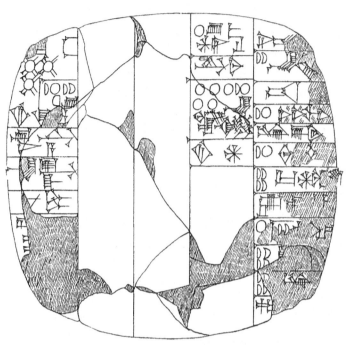

No. 39

Reverse

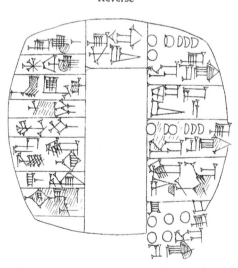

Plate 67

No. 40

Obverse

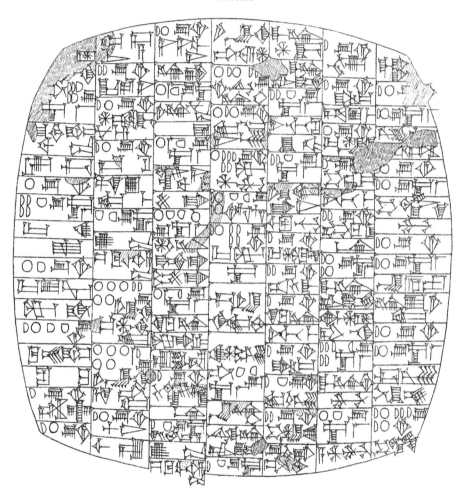

Plate 68

No. 40

Reverse

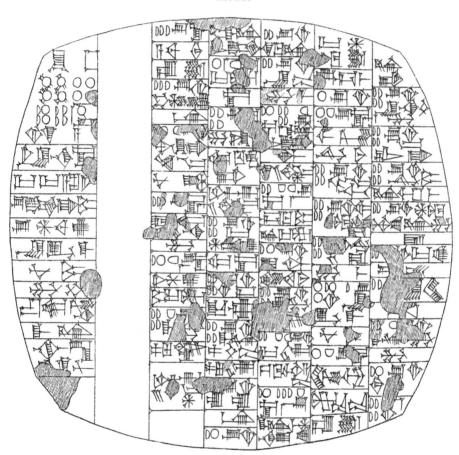

Plate 69

No. 41

Obverse

Reverse

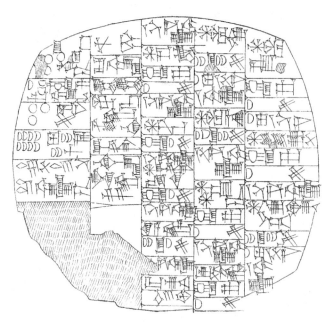

Plate 70

No. 42

Obverse

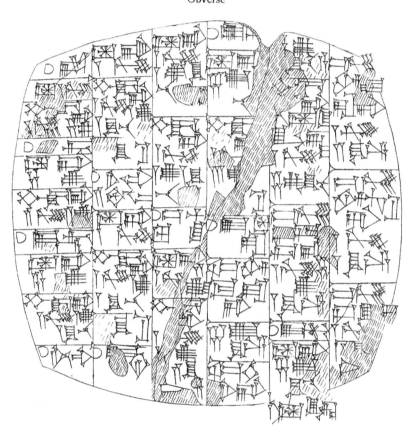

Plate 71

No. 42

Reverse

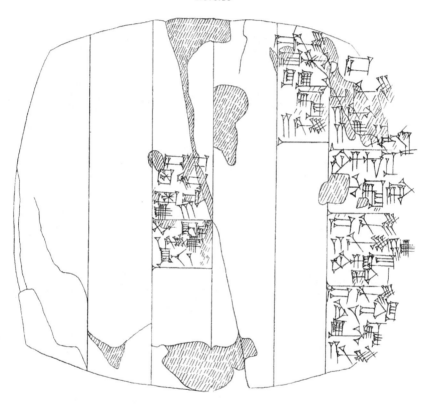

Plate 72

No. 43

Obverse

Reverse

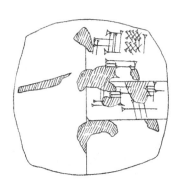

No. 44

Obverse

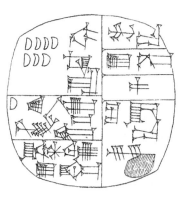

No. 45

Obverse

Reverse

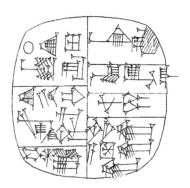

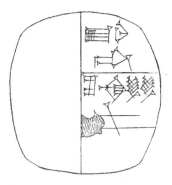

Plate 73

No. 46

Obverse

Reverse

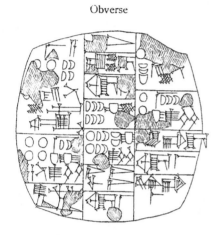

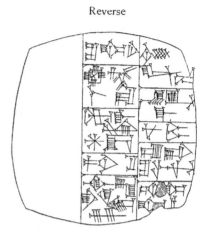

No. 47

Obverse

Reverse

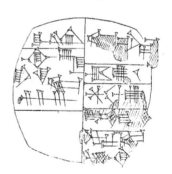

Plate 74

No. 48

Obverse

Reverse

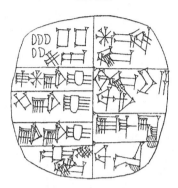

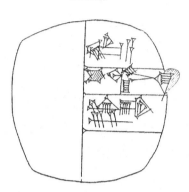

No. 49

Obverse

Reverse

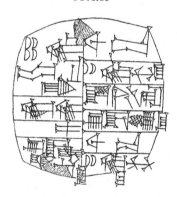

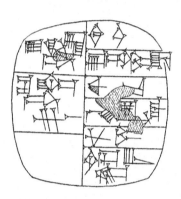

No. 50

Obverse

Reverse

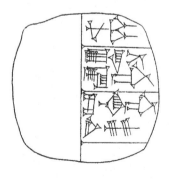

Plate 75

No. 51

Obverse

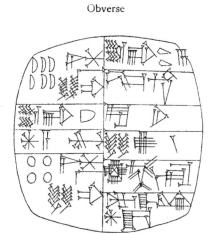

Reverse

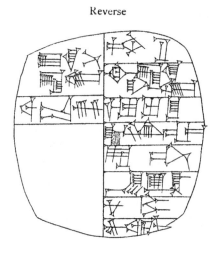

No. 52

Obverse

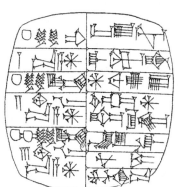

Reverse

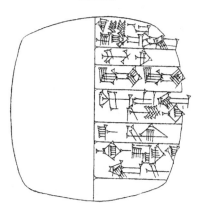

Obverse

No. 46

Obverse   Reverse

Plate 77

No. 42

Obverse

No. 51

Obverse

Reverse

Plate 78

No. 40

Obverse

Plate 79

No. 40

Reverse

No. 35

Obverse

No. 45

Obverse   Reverse

Hussey v

Plate 81

No. 35

Reverse

No. 48

Obverse

Reverse